Winston Churchill

THE MAKING OF A WARLORD

Winston Churchill

THE MAKING OF A WARLORD

ANTHONY TUCKER-JONES

Frontline Books

Published in Great Britain in 2026 by
FRONTLINE BOOKS
An imprint of
Pen & Sword Books Ltd
Yorkshire - Philadelphia

ISBN 978 1 03612 4 489

A CIP catalogue record for this book is available from the British Library.

Book Design by Dominic Allen

Printed and bound in the UK by CPI Group (UK) Ltd, Croydon, CR0 4YY

The Publisher's authorised representative in the EU for product safety is
Authorised Rep Compliance Ltd., Ground Floor, 71 Lower Baggot Street, Dublin D02 P593, Ireland.
www.arccompliance.com

For a complete list of Pen & Sword titles please contact
PEN & SWORD BOOKS LIMITED
47 Church Street, Barnsley, South Yorkshire, S70 2AS, England
E-mail: enquiries@pen-and-sword.co.uk
Website: www.pen-and-sword.co.uk
or
PEN AND SWORD BOOKS
1950 Lawrence Road, Havertown, PA 19083, USA
E-mail: uspen-and-sword@casematepublishers.com
Website: www.penandswordbooks.com

Contents

Introduction

'It is the misfortune of a good many Members [of Parliament] to encounter in our daily walks an increasing number of persons armed with cameras to take pictures for the illustrated Press which is so rapidly developing,' grumbled Winston Churchill on 26 June 1911 to a fellow parliamentarian. At the time, he was serving as the Home Secretary and the newspapers were giving him a very hard time over his controversial handling of the Siege of Sidney Street in London and the Tonypandy riots in Wales. Being photographed and filmed, apparently taking personal charge of the former operation, had drawn a lot of criticism. The press felt the Home Secretary running around like some junior officer was not the becoming conduct of a very senior government official. He was held personally responsible for the army firing a rather excessive sounding 500 rounds of ammunition, and causing the police hardship because he let the siege drag on. In the case of the Welsh riots, Lord Northcliffe's *The Times* newspaper attacked him for not using troops against the rioters.

Churchill, though, was hardly in a position to be anti-press as he had made very good money as a war correspondent in Cuba, India, and South Africa with the

Daily Graphic, Daily Telegraph, Indian Pioneer, and *The Morning Post*. He then used the press to publicise his books based on his foreign adventures and his reporting. Winston learned the power of a good photo when he was photographed, hands on hips, addressing an enthusiastic crowd outside Durban town hall on 23 December 1899 following his dramatic escape from Boer captivity in Pretoria. He then returned to the scene of his capture and made sure he was photographed there. This coverage undoubtedly helped him get elected as a member of parliament the following year. However, when he defected from the Conservatives to the Liberals in May 1904, in opposition to government attempts to curb Jewish immigration, his radical politics were mercilessly lampooned by the Tory press.

Photos of him fraternising with Kaiser Wilhelm II in Germany in 1906 and again in 1909 were perhaps not quite so prudent as those taken in South Africa. His first visit was splashed across the front page of the *Daily Mirror*, and some felt that he was nothing more than an entitled upstart mixing with foreign royalty. Churchill, though, always gave as good as he got when it came to press criticism. On 18 May 1907, he attacked the newspapers as, 'A mischief-making Press, eavesdropping, misrepresenting, dealing in word-pictures'. Shortly after when he was appointed President of the Board of Trade the *Daily Mirror, Daily News* and the *Star* were all extravagantly singing his praises. 'If prophecy were ever safe, it would be safe to predict that Mr Winston Churchill - soldier, war correspondent, traveller, biographer ...' wrote the *Daily Mirror*, 'will one day, and not that far hence, attain the Premiership.' Churchill was wise not to let such fortune telling fuel his ego.

When he was First Lord of the Admiralty, he told the House of Commons on 7 August 1914, 'We wish to deal with the newspaper Press in such a way as to enable the people of this country to follow what is taking place reasonably and intelligibly. It is on information of that kind that panic and unnecessary alarm can best be avoided.' His enthusiasm for the press though, was severely tempered by the extreme mauling he received over his failed Gallipoli campaign the following year. The press branded him 'a danger to this country'. His wife, Clementine, was so alarmed by the backlash she noted, 'the Dardanelles haunted him for the rest of his life. He always believed in it. When he left the Admiralty, he thought he was finished. I thought he would never get over the Dardanelles; I thought he would die of grief.'

COURTING FLEET STREET

Churchill never seemed to worry about the clash of interest working as a journalist, while a soldier and then a politician. His high-profile journalistic activities while in uniform contributed to the War Office eventually forbidding officers from moonlighting. He very actively courted the press barons of Fleet Street in London as a source of regular income and as political allies. He partly did this through the dining society known as The Other Club which he co-founded in 1911. Conveniently, its members included the newspaper proprietors, Lords Beaverbrook, Camrose, and Rothermere.

Churchill, in the aftermath of Gallipoli, cultivated a close friendship with Lord Beaverbrook, who owned the *Daily Express*. The latter became the most successful mass circulation newspaper in the world. Beaverbrook also ended up owning the *Evening Standard* and the *Sunday Express*. Towards the end of the First World War, he briefly served as Minister of Information, which put him in charge of propaganda. Just before the outbreak of the Second World War, the *Evening Standard* on 4 July 1939 reported there was, 'an immense movement now to put Mr Churchill in Government.' The paper added that the campaign was aided by a 'terrific barrage from the newspaper artillery'. Although Beaverbrook and Churchill had occasional major fallings out, he proved to be a staunch ally of Winston's, especially during the Second World War. Winston noted, 'on the whole a relationship had been maintained which was a warm personal friendship, which had subsisted through all the vicissitudes of the past.' Beaverbrook would ably serve Churchill as Minister of Aircraft Production and Minister of Supply during the Second World War.

Churchill and Lord Northcliffe, the founder of the *Daily Mail* and *Daily Mirror*, were normally on good terms. Indeed one of Churchill's prized possessions was a small white china bust of Napoleon Bonaparte given to him by Northcliffe. However, in 1916 he returned it after Northcliffe personally offended him by joking he was seeking to take David Lloyd George's job as Minister of Munitions. This was the final straw as Northcliffe's papers had reported extensively and critically on the Allies' failure at Gallipoli. At the time Churchill was desperate to return to government after resigning as First Lord of the Admiralty and his stint in the trenches. Northcliffe wrote to apologise, 'The attitude of my public newspapers toward public men has nothing to do with my private disposition toward individuals. Had I thought that the remark would have wounded you, I would not for a moment have made it.' Churchill accepted the apology and his gift back. Northcliffe died six years later.

Churchill was also friends with Northcliffe's brother, Lord Rothermere, who subsequently took over the *Daily Mail* and *Daily Mirror*. The pair fell out over Gallipoli as Rothermere supported his brother's call for the Allied withdrawal. Churchill, though, continued to happily write for the *Daily Mail*. When he was serving as Chancellor of the Exchequer, he criticised Rothermere for supporting Liberal leader David Lloyd George's proposed public spending. 'Lord Rothermere, chief author of the anti-waste campaign,' said Winston in his Budget speech on 15 April 1929, 'has enlisted under the Happy Warrior of Squandermania.' Rothermere, at the end of 1935, mischievously bet Churchill £2,000 that he could not abstain from alcohol for a year. 'I refused as I think life would not be worth living,' Winston ruefully told Clementine.

Similarly, he was friendly with Lord Camrose, the owner of the *Daily Telegraph* and the *Sunday Times*. Camrose serialised Churchill's Duke of Marlborough biography and published articles by him before the war, once his work for the *Evening Standard* dried up. In the summer of 1939, Camrose led an unsuccessful campaign in the *Daily Telegraph* to get Churchill appointed to prime minister

Neville Chamberlain's Cabinet. He even lobbied Chamberlain personally. A huge poster, paid for by an anonymous supporter, was put up on the Strand in London asking, 'What Price Churchill?' Further pressure was brought to bear by the *Daily Mirror, Manchester Guardian, News Chronicle, Observer,* and *Yorkshire Post.* Chamberlain was not receptive, and it took the outbreak of war to achieve Churchill's rehabilitation.

Churchill socialised with newspaper proprietor Lord Riddell, who owned the *News of the World.* He made money writing for him. Riddell enjoyed Churchill's confidence and frankness. After losing his position at the Admiralty in 1915, Churchill dramatically informed Riddell, 'I am finished.' Riddell was taken aback when Winston was indiscreet about his relationship with the other press barons. On one occasion, he was shocked when Churchill read out a cable 'from his friend Northcliffe, with whom he was now upon terms of intimate association.' Riddell felt it inappropriate for Churchill to be quite so open about his business arrangements.

Churchill meticulously kept press-cutting books containing his own voluminous output as well as reports about him. The latter included a cutting from the *Palestine Weekly* when he was Secretary of State for the Colonies, attending the Cairo Conference in 1921. It recounted to Churchill's embarrassment how he had been thrown while out camel riding with the war hero Lawrence of Arabia.

Mary Soames, the youngest of Winston and Clementine's five children, was likewise an enthusiastic chronicler who, from 1939 at the age of seventeen, collected eighteen scrapbooks about her parents' exploits. The Churchill children also had to learn to cope with the celebrity that their family name continuously attracted. On 24 June 1925, daughters Diana, Sarah, and Mary featured on the cover of *The Tatler* for all to see.

The following year, Churchill, in the brief absence of the national press due to the General Strike, even ran his own short-lived government newspaper. He edited the *British Gazette* and wrote much of the content. Its circulation peaked at about two million. In his role as editor, he made it clear he was not in favour of reconciliation with the trade unions, who were striking over wage cuts. One headline read, 'No

Flinching'. Many did not forgive his hardline stance. The *Daily Mail*, though, after praising the fortitude of Prime Minister Stanley Baldwin in confronting the strike, added, 'Nor can the services of Winston Churchill be overlooked. His energy and initiative have never been more clearly shown in a great cause.'

Churchill was well aware of the value of the visual media as a potential marketing tool — especially when it came to selling himself either as a soldier, journalist, author, or politician. He became an advocate of the adage that, 'A picture is worth a thousand words.' The use of photographs was revolutionised with the development of the wirephoto in the 1920s, which permitted the instantaneous transmission of images. It was done by scanning photographic prints and converting them into audio tones. These were transmitted over dedicated phone lines to create a silver gelatin photographic support that could be processed in a dark room. Associated Press launched its wirephoto service in the mid-1930s. Throughout his life, Churchill was regularly pursued by newspaper staff photographers, news agency photographers, and freelancers. On the whole, he cultivated a good relationship with them.

He was, though, sensitive to photographs being used as a weapon against him. On 4 June 1929, when he was the outgoing Chancellor of the Exchequer, he was stung by the left-wing *Daily Herald* when it published a photograph showing him carrying a book provocatively titled 'War'. The caption read, 'Mr Churchill arriving in Downing Street with a book on one of his favourite subjects — "War".' It was actually an anti-war novel, but he was unhappy at the suggestion he was a warmonger and wrote angrily to the editor claiming the photo was a fake. It was not, though the title had been enhanced by the paper. Churchill refused to apologise, having an active dislike for the *Daily Herald*.

MOVING PICTURES

As he grew older, Churchill learned how to play the game with the press. It could, as he well knew, be a merciless opponent or a useful ally. In later life, he employed the expression, 'The Power of the Press — and of the Suppress'. Professor Richard Toye says of him in his book *A Life in the News: Winston Churchill*, 'As an instinctive showman and one of the first politicians to be a true global celebrity, he exploited the media (including the new technologies of radio and film) to spectacular effect.'

At one point, a film career even beckoned. While in Hollywood in 1929, Churchill befriended British silent movie star Charlie Chaplin. Churchill liked him greatly, though was not so keen on his left-wing politics. Chaplin recalled on their first meeting that Churchill appeared, 'Napoleon-like with his hand in his waistcoat'. This led to a conversation about Napoleon, who, Churchill admired, and his comedic potential. Their encounter wetted Winston's appetite to get involved in the lucrative business of movie making. A couple of years later, Chaplin, who was in London for a movie premiere, spent the weekend with Churchill at Chartwell. Winston called him 'the great man' and found him highly entertaining at the dinner table. During a tour of the house, the pair discussed the possibility of Chaplin making a comedy about young Napoleon. Churchill, who had many books on him, hoped that Chaplin would commission him to write a script. Nothing, though, came of it.

Churchill cultivated a relationship with the British film industry, in particular, director and producer Alexander Korda. They shared a romantic vision of British history. This led to Churchill's next attempt at script writing. Korda commissioned him to produce a script about the reign of King George V, which Korda wanted to release for the silver jubilee in 1935. Rather optimistically, Winston told Clementine, 'I have no doubt that the film will be a commercial success'. It and another script about the First World War by Churchill never got made, but he was paid for them and Korda paid him an annual retainer just in case. In truth, neither script was very good.

Korda produced a series of stirring historical epics which Churchill greatly admired. As a veteran of the Battle of Omdurman, he was a fan of Korda's *Four Feathers* set in the Sudan in the 1890s and *Lady Hamilton* about British naval hero Lord Horatio Nelson. The latter film reduced him to tears. Martin Gilbert, Churchill's official biographer, wrote, 'Churchill had always loved films and became something of an addict.' Chips Gemmell, who worked as part of Churchill's secretarial team in the late 1950s, recalled, 'He loved the films, any film.'

Churchill reportedly showed *Lady Hamilton* repeatedly on HMS *Prince of Wales* during the Atlantic conference in August 1941. The following summer, Labour politician Aneurin Bevan spread a scurrilous rumour that Churchill, in return for a large fee as a historical adviser on *Lady Hamilto*n and *The Young Mr Pitt*, had promised Korda a knighthood. Certainly, he had some input with both films as he saw parallels between Nelson and Pitt standing up to Napoleon and his position regarding Hitler. 'There was the long struggle against Napoleon,' he wrote, 'in which our survival was secured through the domination of the seas by the British Navy under the classic leadership of Nelson and his associates.' He viewed this achievement in terms of the desperate Battle of the Atlantic.

Churchill greatly appreciated the propaganda value of Korda's historical movies in America prior to Pearl Harbor, which showed Britain as a plucky nation that was never prepared to give in. After the Second World War, Korda paid a large sum for the film rights of Churchill's *The History of the English-Speaking Peoples*, again no movie went into production. He also put Churchill's actress daughter, Sarah, under contract, though this did not bear fruit either.

Churchill's favourite actor was Charles Laughton, who won an Oscar in 1933 for his leading role in *The Private Life of Henry VIII*. The latter was directed by Alexander Korda. Churchill liked Laughton's portrayal of Nero in Cecil B. DeMille's *The Sign of the Cross*. Laughton bore a passing resemblance to Churchill, and it is quite possible that Winston was influenced by Laughton's pugnacious expressions.

During the war, Churchill regularly showed movies at Chequers, the prime minister's official country residence. Both Korda's London Films production company and Metro-Goldwyn-Mayer pioneered renting films to the wealthy who had the luxury of their own screening rooms. Considering the immense stress that Churchill was under, he no doubt found movies relaxing and a source of inspiration. Air Marshal Sir Arthur Harris, commander of RAF Bomber Command, on attending Winston's movie nights observed, 'One realised, of course, that he was really resting himself in this atmosphere and that his thoughts were often far away. Sometimes one could hear him rehearse a phrase for a telegram he would send later.'

Although Churchill was a movie fan, this did not prevent him from seeking to ban a film during the war that he considered unpatriotic. When he learned that the script for *The Life and Death of Colonel Blimp* was about an ageing, very set in his ways Home Guard soldier who had fought in the Boer War and the First World he thought it was poking fun at him. The inspiration was actually cartoonist David Low's character Colonel Blimp, who first appeared in Lord Beaverbrook's London *Evening Standard* in 1934 and Lieutenant General Douglas Brownrigg, who acted as military adviser for the film.

Churchill wrote to Brendan Bracken, the Minister of Information, asking, 'Pray propose to me the measures necessary to stop this foolish production before it gets any further.' Bracken was not keen on suppressing it and pointed out that he did not have the authority to do so. Churchill's intervention was sparked by James Grigg, Secretary of State for War, who first raised concerns that the script might be damaging to the British Army. Following a viewing of the completed film by the Ministry of Information and the War Office, it was released on 10 June 1943. Churchill watched it the night before at a special screening and reportedly enjoyed it. The movie did come under attack in the press for featuring sympathetic German characters. Notably, it was not screened in America until 1945 on Churchill's instructions.

Churchill understood the media could act as a valuable mouthpiece, especially when it came to holding the government to account. 'There is an extraordinary volume of German propaganda in this country,' he warned the House of Commons on 26 March 1936, 'of mis-statements made on the highest authority — which everyone knows could be easily disproved — but which obtain currency.' He then went on to castigate government ministers for not doing more to disabuse the public.

Winston must have been extremely flattered when, shortly after, on 11 May 1936, the *Daily Mail*, in response to Hitler's militarisation of the Rhineland, ran a piece called 'Why Not Mr. Churchill?' In it, special correspondent F.G. Prince-White wrote, 'To younger students of politics it is a most puzzling mystery that Mr. Churchill was not Prime Minister long ago. They look at his record and discover that he has occupied almost every other Government position.' Prince-White then went on to list all his ministerial roles over the years, adding, 'Here is no mediocre experience, but such as might well stand a Prime Minister in good stead.'

Throughout the 1930s, the press could not understand how it was that Churchill, relegated to the back benches in the House of Commons, seemed so well informed about German rearmament. On 23 July 1936, the *Daily Record and Mail* published a humorous four-pane cartoon showing him being passed secrets on the street by a tramp, at a club by a socialite, at sea by a submariner, and in bed by a pigeon. Little did they know that Desmond Morton, the Head of the Industrial Intelligence Centre at the War Office, was regularly leaking classified reports to Churchill.

Just before the Second World War commenced, Churchill told the House of Commons on 13 April 1939, 'We sneer at the Press, but they give an extremely true picture of a great deal that is going on, a very much fuller and more detailed picture than we are able to receive from ministers of the Crown.' When he became prime minister in May 1940, he would harness the media to assist with Britain's war effort and to disseminate propaganda. 'I must say, quite frankly,' he confessed to the House of Commons, 'that I hold it perfectly justifiable to deceive the enemy even if at the same time your own people are for a while misled.'

Churchill, despite being a champion of free speech, became an enthusiastic supporter of wartime censorship, which his colleagues had to temper on occasion. In one instance, though, they fully supported him. During the critical Battle of the Atlantic, shipping losses were such that he became very sensitive about how they were reported in the newspapers. Philip Zec, a political cartoonist employed by the *Daily Mirror*, on 6 March 1942, had a cartoon published depicting a merchant seaman desperately clinging to the wreckage of a ship. The implication was that the vessel had been torpedoed by a German U-boat. The caption declared, 'The price of petrol has been increased by one penny — Official.' Churchill and his ministers were angered by the suggestion that oil companies were profiting from the hard-pressed Atlantic convoys. He also thought it was a deliberate attempt to sabotage morale and became convinced Zec, who had Russian parents, was some sort of fifth columnist.

Herbert Morrison, Minister of Supply, no doubt at Churchill's urging, wrote to Cecil Thomas, the paper's editor, to complain, and the matter was raised in the House of Commons. Morrison told the House, 'The cartoon in question is only one example, but a particularly evil example, of the policy and methods of a newspaper which, intent on exploiting an appetite for sensation and with a reckless indifference to the national interest and to the prejudicial effect on the war effort, has repeatedly published scurrilous misrepresentations'. Thomas found himself branded unpatriotic for passing the cartoon for publication, and the paper was threatened with closure. Zec argued he meant it to be a warning about profiteering and wasting precious fuel in the light of the terrible sacrifices being made to ship it to Britain. Nonetheless, Churchill instructed MI5 to look into Zec's political affiliations. The *Daily Mirror*'s shareholders were similarly investigated. Nothing untoward was discovered, but Zec was very publicly and unfairly accused of being a traitor.

The affair seemed to have the desired result. Churchill told the House of Commons in November 1942, 'There is a great advantage, I think, in our not publishing the shipping losses.' He went on to praise all those involved in such operations for avoiding careless talk. Churchill then added, 'A tribute is also due to the Press for the extreme discretion which they practised, and which they were asked to practice, in avoiding all speculation upon dangerous topics... Democracies have to show that they are not incapable of keeping their war secrets.'

NEVER CAMERA SHY

The title of this book is self-explanatory; Winston is, after all, one of the most photographed individuals in history. The aim is to provide insight into the man as a soldier and wartime leader through pictures of his many remarkable exploits and the events he was involved in. Mary Soames first encapsulated his relationship with the camera in her book *Family Album: A Personal Selection from Four Generations of Churchills*. Clementine Churchill created eight haphazard volumes of family photos, and Mary recalled, 'She also possessed various presentation albums of special occasions, and many wartime (1939-45) photographs come from albums of official photographs'.

Churchill appreciated the power of a photo and was always ready with a pose. He cultivated a dress style that helped him stand out; this included signature props such as a cigar, which was rarely out of his hand, walking stick, and hat. On one memorable occasion the prop was a gangster's 'Tommy' gun. Sometimes his attire seemed slightly old-fashioned or plain eccentric, such as his distinctive one-piece Siren suits, which again help him to stand out. His family dubbed the latter 'rompers', as in baby clothes. Furthermore, he was not shy about wearing military uniforms when he felt that the occasion justified it.

There is no denying that Churchill, although by no means a handsome man, proved to be highly photogenic. The camera loved him, and he instinctively knew how to strike a stance that reinforced his statesmanship. While he could look rather intimidating, he was never shy of giving a mischievous smile. It was Armenian-Canadian photographer Yousuf Karsh who captured the world's lasting impression of a pugnacious Churchill with his famous portrait, *The Roaring Lion*, taken on 30 December 1941. This iconic photo encapsulated Churchill's look of almost menacing defiance, his beady eyes daring the viewer to challenge his resolve. There is a story behind how Karsh achieved Churchill's belligerent expression, but more of that later. Since then, *The Roaring Lion* has adorned everything from mugs to t-shirts. One of Karsh's final photos of Churchill, published on the front of the *Daily Sketch*'s tribute to him issued on 30 January 1965, was far less flattering.

Churchill, though, had already been cultivating his now famous wartime 'bulldog' expression as his public persona. English photographer Cecil Beaton encapsulated it to perfection in the photograph he took of Winston in the Cabinet Room in September 1940. Beaton subsequently gained Churchill's approval by travelling to Burma as a Ministry of Information photographer to record British military operations there. Sarah Churchill, who served in the Women's Auxiliary Air Force during the war, noted, 'Though I have had many things to say about the press in my life, the war correspondents and the frontline journalists and photographers who recorded the fighting always deserve a special mention.' She was trained by the Royal Air Force as a photographic interpreter, examining aerial reconnaissance photos, which was highly specialised and top-secret work. She later married Antony Beauchamp, another cameraman who covered the war in Burma. He turned out to be one photographer Winston and Clementine took an instant disliking to.

It is worth highlighting that Churchill was regularly photographed from birth. Thanks to the work of British inventor William Fox Talbot and British chemist John Herschel, the Victorians quickly embraced photography. Portrait photographers became very popular amongst the wealthy. War photography also first came into its own during the Victorian era. Key amongst the early war photographers were Roger Fenton and James Robertson, who recorded the horrors of the Crimean War with their rudimentary cameras.

Winston was first photographed as a fresh-faced baby and again, most memorably, aged two, five, and seven. After that, there was no stopping him, and he seemed to get his photo taken at every available opportunity. He had an uncanny knack of ensuring his expression made him stand out even in a crowd. The resulting plethora of images means it is possible to chart every major career milestone visually.

Notably, on the eve of the Second World War, Churchill was interviewed about the international situation by Stefan Lorant, the Hungarian founding editor of the newly launched magazine *Picture Post*. This publication pioneered photojournalism and proved an immediate success. The interview took place on 3 February 1939 at Chartwell, where Churchill was photographed by German-born photographer Kurt Hutton at work in his study, wandering the grounds and bricklaying. Churchill subsequently featured in a series of illustrated *Picture Post* articles that, rather timely, reminded the British public of his stance on Nazi Germany. On 29 April 1940, just before he became prime minister, his portrait appeared on the cover of the American magazine *Life* with the simple caption 'Britain's Warlord.' In this photo, he employed his 'bulldog' expression to full effect. There could be no denying that Churchill was qualified and ready to step in to help his country in its hour of need.

THE WAR LEADER

Churchill fully harnessed the power of photography to portray himself as a war leader. This was especially the case during the Second World War, when serving as prime minister, he was always thirsting to visit his generals and troops at the front. Likewise, he revelled in having his picture taken with the world's leaders, particularly as a member of the Big Three. On visits to the front, Churchill was invariably shadowed by members of the Army Film and Photographic Unit. This famously produced the documentary feature films *Desert Victory*, *Tunisian Victory*, and *Burma Victory*, which proved popular with him. If he was visiting American units, the task fell to the combat cameramen or war correspondents of the US Army Signal Corps, who were deployed by the Signal Corps Photographic Center.

Although Churchill was always very happy to be the centre of attention throughout the war, on at least one occasion, he objected vigorously. British and American soldiers following the Allied victory in Tunisia were gathered in the Roman amphitheatre at Carthage for his address on 1 June 1943. When he mounted the stage, he was greeted by rapturous cheering and, for a second, was taken aback by the overwhelming reception. He immediately wanted the crowd captured for prosperity, and his eyes alighted on a young Lieutenant Alan Whicker from the AFPU in front of him, holding a camera.

'Get a picture of that. Don't take me, take that,' instructed Churchill, pointing at the roaring multitude. Whicker hesitated, wanting to explain that there were cameramen posted behind Churchill doing just that. His job was to get close-up shots of the prime minister. Annoyed, Churchill once more demanded, 'Get a picture of that.' Still, Whicker hesitated, and at that point, Lieutenant General Kenneth Anderson, commander of the British First Army, stepped forward and very firmly ordered, 'Take a picture of that!' The photograph was duly taken by the very chastised Whicker. He later got his own iconic shot of the prime minister. Churchill very obligingly took off his sun helmet, which he placed on the end of his walking stick and held it aloft with a dramatic flourish.

On the home front, Churchill was relentless in touring Britain's bombed cities to see the damage firsthand and, equally, to help boost civilian morale. In Britain's media war, Churchill began to defiantly use the V for Victory gesture using his index and middle fingers. This again provided many iconic images of him. When the Second Front opened in Normandy in mid-1944, it was all those around him could do to prevent him being physically involved in the D-Day landings and then later with the Rhine Crossing. Instead, Churchill had to be content with being a VIP war tourist, often to the mild irritation of the Allied commanders, especially the long-suffering Field Marshal Bernard Montgomery, who dreaded his visits. Churchill loved being at the front and always ensured he was photographed amongst the troops like the true war leader he was.

HATES THE MICROPHONE

While Churchill greatly enjoyed writing, public speaking, and was a fan of film and photography, he did not always enjoy being on the radio. 'How I wish Winston would not talk on the wireless unless he is feeling in good form,' noted Labour politician Harold Nicolson in his diary on 19 June 1940. 'He hates the microphone, and when we bullied him into speaking last night, he just sulked and read his House of Commons ['finest hour'] speech again... it sounded ghastly on the radio. All the great vigour he put into it seemed to evaporate.' Nicolson made a similar observation on 27 March 1944, 'People seem to think Winston's broadcast last night was that of a worn and petulant old man. I am sickened by the absence of gratitude towards him.'

Nor did Churchill embrace the new technology of television. 'The curious fact that the House [of Commons] prefers to give two days to the television White Paper and only one day to foreign affairs,' he said in 1953, 'may be noted by future historians as an example of a changing sense of proportion in modern thought.' How astute he was in light of the impending age of fatuous television celebrity. He opposed televising Queen Elizabeth II's coronation at Westminster Abbey that year on the grounds that it should not be presented 'as if it were a theatrical performance.' The Queen overruled him. Churchill though through incredible hard work and dedication, as well as being his own prototype spin-doctor, ensured that he became one of the most famous and recognisable historical figures of the Twentieth Century. In part he had the media to thank for that.

CHAPTER ONE

The Early Years

1874–1895

Winston Churchill, although born into privilege, was not born into wealth. His father, as the third son of the 7th Duke of Marlborough, was never in line to inherit the dukedom or Blenheim Palace. Churchill, like every one of his class, had a conventional childhood, which involved being raised by a nanny and then packed off to boarding school as soon as possible. His school days were not very happy, and he failed to apply himself. However, he grew up against a backdrop of constant Victorian wars, which helped spur him on to join the army. It was not until he went to Sandhurst Military Academy that he began to find his stride and enjoyed military life. In the early photographs of him, he exhibits a rather haughty expression that he would deploy in later life to great effect, culminating in *The Roaring Lion*. After Churchill was commissioned into the 4th Queen's Own Hussars, he seemed to show a new-found confidence and sense of purpose. On sabbatical from his regiment, he travelled to Cuba as a war correspondent. This sparked his lifelong career in journalism.

The young couple. Winston Churchill's parents, Lord and Lady Randolph Churchill, by French photographer George Penabert at the time of their marriage in Paris. His father, at age 24, married 20-year-old American heiress Jeanette 'Jennie' Jerome on 15 April 1874. They first met during a sailing regatta on the Isle of Wight the previous year.

Lord Randolph Henry Spencer-Churchill (13 February 1849 — 24 January 1895) was the third son of the 7th Duke of Marlborough and Lady Frances Vane. Shortly before Churchill's birth, his father was elected as the member of parliament for Woodstock. Randolph went on to serve as Chancellor of the Exchequer, Leader of the House of Commons and Secretary of State for India in Lord Salisbury's Government. His political career had a profound effect on young Winston.

Jennie Jerome (9 January 1854 – 29 June 1921) was nineteen when she met Lord Randolph at a ball on the frigate HMS *Ariadne*. Winston Churchill wrote, 'She shone for me like the Evening Star — I loved her dearly, but at a distance.' His relationship with her would become much closer after his father's untimely death at the age of forty-five in 1895.

The illustrious Churchill name was to open many doors for young Winston. John Churchill (1650–1722), the 1st Duke of Marlborough, was an accomplished general and political player. He won victories in Europe at Blenheim, Ramillies, Oudenaarde and Malplaquet during the War of Spanish Succession (1701–1714). Winston would develop a fascination for John Churchill, culminating in his multi-volume biography on the duke. John's strategy against King Louis XIV of France would greatly inspire Winston's war against Adolf Hitler over 200 years later.

John Churchill and his wife Sarah Jennings were elevated to the Duke and Duchess of Marlborough by Queen Anne to mark his victory over the French at Blenheim in 1704. They were also gifted an estate at Woodstock, outside Oxford, where they built Blenheim Palace. Winston was born there on 30 November 1874. His parents had intended that he be delivered at their London home, but Winston arrived six weeks early while they were staying at Blenheim. *The Times* reported in its births section on 1 December 1874, 'On 30 Nov, at Blenheim Palace, the Lady RANDOLPH CHURCHILL, prematurely, of a son.' During his lifetime, Winston would be a regular guest at Blenheim, staying with his cousin Charles Spencer-Churchill, the 9th Duke of Marlborough.

Winston was born during the reign of Queen Victoria, the second-longest-reigning British monarch, who was on the throne for almost sixty-four years (1857–1901). An act of Parliament in 1876 also granted her the title of Empress of India. The British Empire was at its height during her reign, and Winston was very much a child of the Empire. Throughout the Victorian era, the British Army was involved in over sixty military campaigns involving at least 400 battles across five continents.

As a young boy, Winston was bombarded with constant news coverage of Queen Victoria's far-flung campaigns. In 1879, Britain became embroiled in the Anglo-Zulu War, and newspapers such as *The Illustrated London News* reported on British military exploits at such places as Isandlwana and Rorke's Drift. The defence of the latter resulted in the award of eleven Victoria Crosses for gallantry, which became an inspiration for schoolboys up and down the land.

Winston, following the British defeat at Isandlwana, wrote, 'I was very angry with the Zulus, and glad to hear they were being killed … After a while it seemed that they were all killed, because this particular war came to an end and there were no more pictures of the Zulus in the papers.' The Zulu army proved incapable of standing up to British firepower. Britain's victory left the country on a deadly collision course with South Africa's Boer population.

A rather haughty-looking Churchill at the age of seven in 1881, wearing a sailor's uniform. Few could have imagined that he would become First Lord of the Admiralty, the political head of the Royal Navy, during both World Wars

That very same year, the British lost the Battle of Majuba Hill in South Africa and the short-lived Transvaal War against the Boers. This sowed the seeds for the subsequent, much longer-lasting and disastrous Boer War, which was to involve Winston.

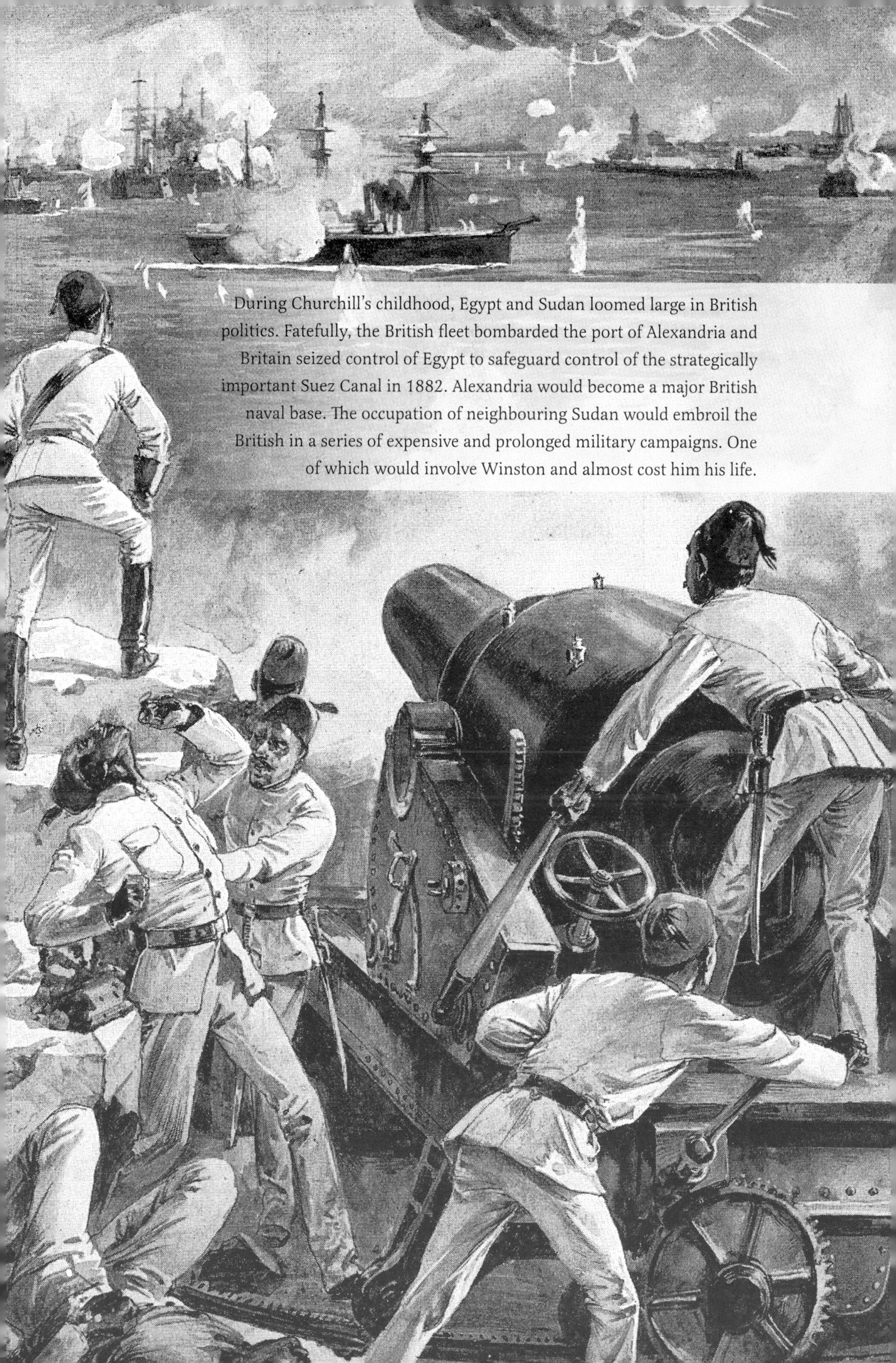

During Churchill's childhood, Egypt and Sudan loomed large in British politics. Fatefully, the British fleet bombarded the port of Alexandria and Britain seized control of Egypt to safeguard control of the strategically important Suez Canal in 1882. Alexandria would become a major British naval base. The occupation of neighbouring Sudan would embroil the British in a series of expensive and prolonged military campaigns. One of which would involve Winston and almost cost him his life.

The British governor of Sudan, Major General Charles Gordon, came under siege at Khartoum in March 1884 during the First Sudan War or Mahdist War. He defied orders to evacuate the city, largely on the grounds that he did not want to get caught on the open road. British media coverage was extensive with *The Illustrated London News* dubbing Gordon 'The Heroic defender of Khartoum.' That April Churchill's school report noted for geography and history, 'Very good, especially history.' However, when it came to general conduct, 'Very bad — is a constant trouble to everybody and is always in some scrape or other.' This essentially was to characterise the rest of his life. Winston was first sent to board at St George's School, Ascot, but was then moved to a boarding school in Brighton, where he was much happier.

A small British force trying to relieve Khartoum formed a defensive square to the north at Abu Klea and fought off a superior Mahdist or Dervish force on 17 January 1885. This engagement was subsequently immortalised by English painter William Barnes Wollen, in which he showed the British square standing fast. Tragically, though, Gordon and his garrison were overwhelmed on 26 January 1885 before help could reach them. His death caused outrage in London and led to calls in Parliament for a punitive expedition to be sent.

British troops arrived at Suakin on the Red Sea to oversee the unsuccessful construction of a railway line to Berber on the Nile north of Atbara. This included the deployment of the newly raised Australian Royal New South Wales regiment. Comprising an infantry battalion and an artillery battery, this was the very first Australian force to serve overseas.

The British presence at Suakin inevitably sparked more fighting in the spring of 1885, and the public, including young Winston, were subjected to highly dramatic images such as these in *The Illustrated London News* based on sketches by artist Walter Paget. The Australians gained their first battle honour at Suakin.

The Illustrated London News reported on the battle of Hasheen in March 1885, which included this stirring illustration of the 5th Lancers scattering Dervish forces. If the ten year old Winston saw this, one can only guess at the impression it made upon his imagination. Even in his wildest dreams, he cannot have conceived he would end up participating in an almost identical lancer charge in Sudan. Like many schoolboys of his era, service in the empire beckoned.

If Winston had picked up *The Illustrated London News* in 1886, he would have been aware that Britain had fought the Third Anglo-Burmese War that year, which brought Burma firmly under the control of the neighbouring British Raj. This was a river war in which Britain had sent a military expedition along the Irrawaddy into Upper Burma. Winston would later serve under one of the Burma veterans on the North-West Frontier. He would also take part in a river war this time involving the Nile.

Churchill was sent to Harrow School as a boarder in April 1888. After his shaky start with the education system, he was grateful, remarking, 'It was from these slender indications of scholarship that [headmaster] Mr. Welldon drew the conclusion that I was worthy to pass into Harrow. It was very much to his credit.' There, Winston gained his first taste of military life. He joined the Harrow School Rifle Corps, which conducted drills that included forming a defensive square and fighting mock battles. Letting young boys loose with rifles and fixed bayonets did not appear to be a health and safety concern at the time. Instead, it was seen as a very good way to prepare them for military service.

A young Winston can be seen clearly in the centre, staring determinedly at the camera. Lord Randolph hoped that his son might study law, but Winston's academic performance was to prove so poor that a career in the military seemed the only real option.

Winston, on the right, photographed in 1889 with his mother and younger brother John Strange Churchill. The latter, better known as Jack, was born in Dublin on 4 February 1880, while Lord Randolph was serving as secretary to John Spencer-Churchill, the 7th Duke of Marlborough, the Lord Lieutenant of Ireland. Jack and Winston would very briefly serve together during the Boer War.

Senior Harrow boys in their distinctive school uniform undergoing drill instruction. Churchill, like many, did not enjoy his time there. 'I am all for Public Schools but I do not want to go there again,' he later wrote. '[Harrow] was an unending spell of worries that did not seem petty.' In the summer of 1888, his house master wrote to Lady Randolph complaining of Winston's 'slovenliness' and warning that if he did not mend his ways, 'he will never make a success of a public school.' Winston had no way of knowing that he would become Harrow's most famous Old Boy.

Winston just managed to pass the entry exam for the Royal Military College, Sandhurst, in 1893. 'It took me three tries to pass into Sandhurst,' he admitted. The following year, he arrived and, rather surprisingly, thrived graduating 20 out of 130 cadets. Lord Randolph wanted his son to join an infantry regiment on the grounds that it would be much cheaper; cavalry officers had to provide their own horses and their groom's uniform. 'My mother explained to him how matters had arranged themselves,' wrote Winston, 'and he seemed quite willing, and even pleased, that I should become a Cavalry Officer.' His father died of syphilis on 24 January 1895, so he could have no further say in the matter. Winston was commissioned as a Second Lieutenant in the 4th Queen's Own Hussars in February 1895. He looks every inch the hussar officer in his full dress or parade uniform. His fur busby is resting on the right-hand arm of his chair.

The traditional ornate hussar jacket is known as a braided dolman. The hussar busby was far from practical; it tended to be top-heavy, especially when wet and dripped rainwater into the eyes. His regiment started life as a dragoon unit in 1685 and took part in the famous charge of the Light Brigade at Balaclava in 1854 during the Crimean War. It became a hussar regiment seven years later.

Winston attired in his regimental service or walking out uniform designed for everyday use. His pillbox forage cap was far more practical than the full-dress busby. Stationed at Aldershot, Hampshire, he was soon bored with barrack life and thirsted for adventure overseas. 'The military year was divided into seven months' summer season of training and five months' winter season of leave, and each officer received a solid block of two and a half months' uninterrupted repose,' he observed. 'All my money had been spent on polo ponies, and as I could not afford to hunt, I searched the world for some scene of adventure or excitement.'

Winston's attention was soon drawn to Cuba, where the locals had risen against Spanish colonial rule. In November 1895, while on extended leave, he and Lieutenant Reginald Barnes sailed to Cuba. There, they joined Spanish forces as unofficial observers and, in Churchill's case, a war correspondent for *The Daily Graphic*. Despite their non-combatant status, they carried firearms.

On his twenty-first birthday, he and Barnes, while accompanying a Spanish column, came under rebel fire and the pair narrowly avoided being shot by the rebels on a number of occasions. On returning home, his reports for *The Daily Graphic* drew condemnation that serving officers should not be involved in other countries' wars. His public criticism of the performance Spanish army also resulted in the displeasure of the Spanish government. Churchill did not mind the media uproar because his adventure had very firmly brought him to the attention of the British public.

CHAPTER TWO

Defender of the Empire

1896–1898

After Churchill returned from Cuba, he and his regiment were sent to help defend the British Raj. Photographs of him in India show a rather callow but enthusiastic-looking youth who enjoyed polo and reading. India was a peacetime deployment, but Churchill, seeking more adventure, managed to get himself assigned to a punitive British expedition on the much-troubled North-West Frontier. After that, he joined another punitive British operation, this time in the Sudan. One of the first things he did when he reached Cairo was to get himself photographed in the uniform of the 21st Lancers, whom he was to serve with. Again, the famous Churchill expression was very much in evidence. Both expeditions saw him acting as a war correspondent, and both were to inspire books setting him firmly on the road to becoming an author.

In 1896, Winston was deployed with the 4th Hussars on peacetime garrison duty to Bangalore in southern India. For something to do, he joined the regimental polo team, having already started playing while a cadet at Sandhurst. Left to right are Albert Savory, Reggie Barnes, who had accompanied Winston to Cuba the previous year, a fresh-faced Churchill, and Reginald Hoare. Winston on 15 October 1896 informed his brother Jack, 'The Polo is very bad — and I expect our subaltern's team will easily beat the whole Bangalore garrison. I have only played three times but have made many goals.' Their matches attracted crowds of up to 9,000 Indians, and his regiment's success became of great interest to Indian newspapers. Churchill thoroughly enjoyed the sport and dubbed it the 'emperor of games'.

In India, he decided to catch up on his education and 'resolved to read history, philosophy and ... I got out the eight volumes of Gibbon's *Decline and Fall of the Roman Empire*.' Edward Gibbon was to have a strong influence on Churchill's own writing style in terms of sweeping narrative and on how he perceived the role of the British Empire. 'I devoured Gibbon,' he recalled. 'I rode triumphantly through it from end to end and enjoyed it all.'

Despite his polo playing, reading, and writing, he was soon thirsting for action. He
sought to escape the confines of his regiment and find a way to reach the remote North-
West Frontier on the border with Afghanistan, where there was regular trouble with the
local tribes. 'Except at harvest-time, when self-preservation enjoins a temporary truce,'
he noted, 'the Pathan tribes are always engaged in private or public war.'

Churchill, in 1897, while on leave in England, learned that the 20,000 Pathan tribesmen
of the Swat Valley on the North-West Frontier had rebelled against British authority.
They trapped two Indian Army regiments in the forts at Chakdara and Malakand.
Although they were relieved, the uprising continued to spread unchecked.

Brigadier General Sir Bindon Blood was placed in command of a punitive operation to quell the rebellion. Churchill got himself assigned to Blood's Malakand Field Force; he also got himself accredited to the *Daily Telegraph* and the *Indian Pioneer* as a war correspondent. Adventure beckoned once more.

When Churchill arrived in early September 1897, Blood instructed him to join Brigadier General P.D. Jeffreys' 2nd Brigade, which consisted of British, Bengali, Punjabi, and Sikh regiments. Churchill soon came to the conclusion that Jeffreys, who had started his military career with the Irish Connaught Rangers and was a veteran of the Zulu War and Third Anglo-Burmese War, was 'a nice man but a bad general'.

'I sent for Churchill and suggested his joining General Jeffreys in order to see a little fighting,' recalled Sir Bindon Blood. 'He was all for it, so I sent him over at once and he saw more fighting than I expected, and very hard fighting too!' The brigade advanced in three columns up the Watelai Valley, but when these became separated, they were ambushed by the Pathans on 16 September 1897.

Sikh soldiers in their large, distinctive turbans on the North-West Frontier. The Malakand Field Force included the 35th and 45th Sikh Infantry regiments. 'The Sikh is the guardian of the marches. He was originally invented to combat the Pathan,' wrote Churchill approvingly.

Churchill, with the 35th Sikh Infantry Regiment, fought near the village of Markhani. The Sikhs, under attack by some 2,000 tribesmen, were forced to retreat. Churchill spent the whole day under fire and fought back using his revolver and then a rifle. 'They kill and mutilate everyone they catch and we do not hesitate to finish off their wounded,' he said. Subsequently, he was attached to the 31st Punjab Infantry Regiment, which saw extensive action.

Resplendent members of the 36th Sikhs photographed in 1897 who were involved in the subsequent Tirah campaign. Churchill was impressed by the Raj's Indian Army, which had only come into being in 1895 with the merger of the forces of Bengal, Bombay, and Madras. In mid-October 1897, Churchill returned to Bangalore and wrote *The Story of the Malakand Field Force*. He dedicated it to: 'Major-General Sir Bindon Blood, K.C.B., under whose command the operations therein recorded were carried out; by whose generalship they were brought to a successful conclusion; and to whose kindness the author is indebted for the most valuable and fascinating experience of his life.'

Churchill's next escapade would take him to Sudan. He was desperately keen to join General Herbert Kitchener's Anglo-Egyptian Army, which in 1896 had been tasked with retaking Khartoum. Kitchener was Sirdar (commander in chief) of the Egyptian Army and was to be appointed Governor General of Sudan once it was retaken.

This contemporary view is looking down the Nile at Khartoum. Kitchener's expedition was intended to secure Sudan and avenge the death of General Charles Gordon some 13 years earlier at the hands of the Mahdists. The latter were determined to oppose the Anglo-Egyptian advance at every turn.

Kitchener's goal was to hoist the British and Egyptian flags over the governor's palace in Khartoum, where General Gordon had been killed. The windows of the building were bricked up by Gordon as part of his defences. First, though, Kitchener had to take the Mahdist capital at Omdurman on the junction of the Blue and White Niles.

Since mid-March 1896, the Anglo-Egyptian Army had been advancing up the Nile from Wadi Halfa by rail and river steamers. The latter were protected by a fleet of armour-plated gunboats. This photograph shows a stern-wheeler river steamer shipping men of the 21st Lancers along the Nile from Aswan to Wadi Halfa, en route to join Kitchener's forces in Sudan. The regiment's horses can be seen standing on both the left and right of the vessel.

Kitchener had defeated the Mahdists at Firket in the summer of 1896, and at the end of the year, he agreed to put Churchill's name down for service with the Egyptian Army. Churchill, who was due three months' leave, considered stopping off in Cairo and presenting himself to Kitchener. Instead, he had got himself assigned to the Malakand Field Force.

By the summer of 1897, Kitchener had fought his way to Berber. He defeated the Mahdists to the south at Atbara on 8 April 1898. Kitchener is in discussion with the Commander of the British Brigade on the Nile, Major General Sir William Gatacre.

At this stage, Churchill began to fret that the war would be over before he could get to the Sudan. However, Kitchener still had to retake Khartoum, and Churchill was confident that Atbara was not the end of the campaign. He knew he had to get to Cairo as soon as possible if he was not to miss out on the action. Winston arrived there on 2 August 1898 with a commission to write for *The Morning Post* and a secondment to the 21st Lancers. While in Cairo, he had this portrait taken.

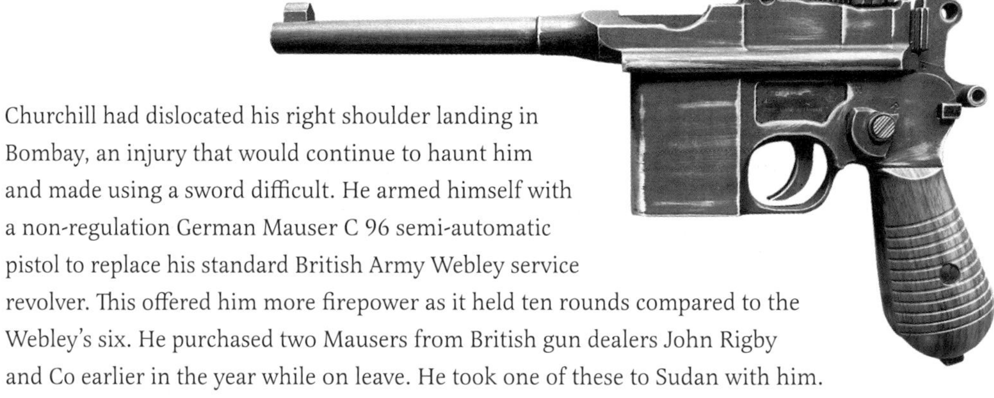

Churchill had dislocated his right shoulder landing in Bombay, an injury that would continue to haunt him and made using a sword difficult. He armed himself with a non-regulation German Mauser C 96 semi-automatic pistol to replace his standard British Army Webley service revolver. This offered him more firepower as it held ten rounds compared to the Webley's six. He purchased two Mausers from British gun dealers John Rigby and Co earlier in the year while on leave. He took one of these to Sudan with him.

Churchill made his way south to Atbara with members of the 21st Lancers and made friends with Lieutenants Robert Grenfell and Richard Molyneux. Lionel James of *The Times*, though, noted that Churchill preferred to eat with the journalists rather than his fellow officers. After leaving Atbara, Churchill got lost and endured an anxious night in the desert before rejoining the column.

The 21st Lancers were Kitchener's only British cavalry unit, and they spent much of their time on patrol acting as his eyes and ears. On 1 September 1898, they reported that some 60,000 Mahdists were gathered outside Omdurman. It was clear that battle was imminent.

The following day, the Mahdists attacked Kitchener's 25,000-strong Anglo-Egyptian Army. He anchored his defensive line on the Nile with his back to the river. The main Dervish force soon wilted in the face of his superior firepower, which included breech-loading rifles, machine guns, and artillery.

Kitchener's flanks were protected by gunboats, which were able to shell the approaching Mahdi army. Amongst them was a young naval officer and future Admiral of the Fleet, David Beatty, who commanded the gunboat *Fateh*. Before battle commenced, Beatty had thrown Churchill, who was walking on the riverbank, a bottle of champagne. It transpired that Beatty's father had served in the 4th Hussars.

Further south, British artillery had moved into position on the opposite bank to shell Omdurman's defences. This was intended to prevent the Dervishes from seeking sanctuary in the city should they withdraw. The battle was to be a triumph for British firepower.

Churchill and the rest of the 21st Lancers deployed south of the Anglo-Egyptian positions. Numbering some 310 men, they were ordered to clear the dry river bed called the *Khur Abu Sunt*. They charged what they thought was a small force, but when they reached their objective, they found several thousand Dervishes hiding there.

Winston, using his pistol, fought his squadron through the enemy ranks. He fired ten rounds, killing up to six men at close range. The carnage was terrible as he explained, 'But now from the direction of the enemy there came a succession of grisly apparitions; horses spouting blood, struggling on three legs, men staggering on foot, men bleeding from terrible wounds, fish-hook spears stuck right through them, arms and faces cut to pieces'. The 21st Lancers suffered twenty-one dead and forty-nine wounded. The regiment also lost 119 horses. An exhilarated Winston miraculously went unscathed.

'Thus ended the Battle of Omdurman,' he wrote, 'the most signal triumph ever gained by the arms of science over barbarians.' He said enemy losses were 'ascertained to be 9,700 killed, and wounded variously estimated at from 10,000 to 16,000. There were, besides, 5,000 prisoners.' He was highly critical of how Kitchener treated the wounded Dervishes at Omdurman. He wrote, '[W]hen an army in the field becomes imbued with the idea that the enemy are vermin who encumber the earth, instances of barbarity may easily be the outcome. This unmeasured condemnation is moreover as unjust as it is dangerous and unnecessary... We are told that the British and Egyptian armies entered Omdurman to free the people from the Khalifa's yoke. Never were rescuers more unwelcome.' Kitchener was understandably not happy about such criticism from a lowly lieutenant.

On his return, home Churchill wrote another book, *The River War: An Historical Account of the Reconquest of the Soudan*, which was published in 1899 in two volumes. In it, he warned prophetically about the dangers posed by militant Islam, 'Far from being moribund, Mohammedanism is a militant and proselytizing faith. It has already spread throughout Central Africa, raising fearless warriors at every step; and were it not that Christianity is sheltered in the strong arms of science, the science against which it had vainly struggled, the civilisation of modern Europe might fall, as fell the civilisation of ancient Rome.' Winston, inspired by his father now sought to embark on a political career.

THE RIVER WAR

AN HISTORICAL ACCOUNT OF

THE RECONQUEST OF THE SOUDAN

BY

WINSTON SPENCER CHURCHILL

AUTHOR OF ' THE STORY OF THE MALAKAND FIELD FORCE, 1897'

EDITED BY COL. F. RHODES, D.S.O.

Illustrated by Angus McNeill, Seaforth Highlanders

IN TWO VOLUMES

VOLUME II.

LONGMANS, GREEN, AND CO.

39 PATERNOSTER ROW, LONDON

NEW YORK AND BOMBAY

1899

All rights reserved

CHAPTER THREE

Off to South Africa

1899-1900

Churchill's journalistic activities in Sudan resulted in an ultimatum from the War Office: desist writing or resign his commission. He resigned. After his hopes of becoming a Member of Parliament were dashed, he set off for South Africa to cover the Boer War as a correspondent. Unable to resist the lure of adventure, he ended up getting captured by the Boers in a highly publicised event. This resulted in a photo of him looking extremely defiant as a prisoner of war. His subsequent dramatic escape helped fuel his international fame even further. Rather than return home, he enlisted in a local South African regiment and saw further action, resulting in yet more newspaper reports and books. His enlistment resulted in yet another photograph of him in uniform.

After failing to win a by-election in July 1899 as the Conservative candidate for Oldham, Churchill's next great adventure was in South Africa. In October 1899, the Boers of Transvaal and Orange Free State invaded British-controlled Cape Colony and Natal. Churchill, who had resigned his commission, arrived in Cape Town at the end of the month as a civilian war correspondent for the *Morning Post*. At the time, on a salary of £250 a month, he was the highest-paid journalist to go to war. Despite being a non-combatant, he took with him his trusty Mauser pistol.

This is what confronted the British authorities in South Africa, the tough Afrikaans-speaking Dutch Boers or farmers. These resourceful fighters would initially prove more than a match for British forces. Churchill, on 1 November 1899, wrote, 'For the last three months the Imperial Government has been in the unpleasant position of watching its adversaries grow continually stronger without being able to make adequate counter-preparations. The Boers had the advantage of drawing first blood.'

A feature of the Boer War was the deployment of armoured trains by the British. One such a train, seen here, had been armoured in the railway workshops of Ladysmith just before the town was besieged by the Boers. 'Nothing looks more formidable and impressive than an armoured train;' noted Churchill, 'but nothing is in fact more vulnerable and helpless. It was only necessary to blow up a bridge or culvert to leave the monster stranded, far from home and help, at the mercy of the enemy.' He was to learn this the hard way in yet another of his life-threatening escapades.

Churchill and Captain Aylmer Haldane, with men from the Royal Durban Light Fusiliers and the Durban Light Infantry, undertook a patrol on an armoured train from Estcourt to Chieveley on 15 November 1899. In total, there were about 150 soldiers plus the train crew. On the return journey, they were shelled by the waiting Boers from a nearby hill. 'The iron sides of the truck tanged with a patter of bullets,' said Churchill. While there had been reports of mounted Boers in the area, the ambush came as an unwelcome surprise.

'The Boers held their fire until the train reached that part of the track nearest to their position…' recalled Churchill. 'The Boers had opened fire on us at 600 yards with two large field guns, a Maxim [machine gun] firing small shells in a stream, and from riflemen lying on the ridge.' In an effort to escape, the engine driver employed full steam. However, the Boers had blocked the line with a boulder, which the train hit at speed, and three trucks were derailed.

Churchill immediately took charge of efforts to clear the track, despite the presence of three commissioned officers. At the head of nine men from the Durban Light Infantry, he first cleared the boulder. Then, using the train, Churchill was able to barge the obstructing trucks out of the way. The locomotive and tender carrying ninety men sped to safety; however, sixty others, along with Churchill and Haldane, were captured by the Boers.

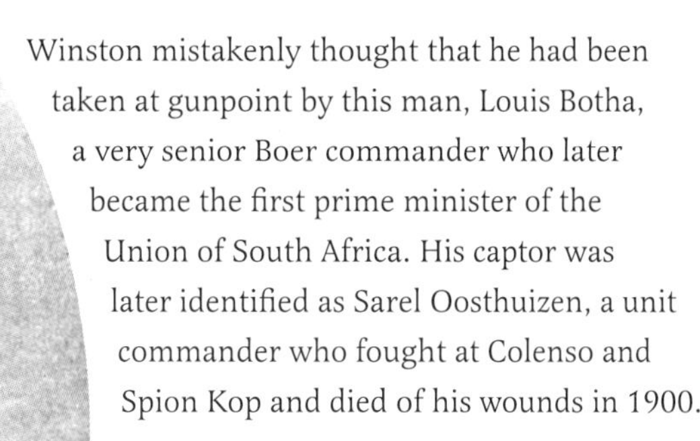

Winston mistakenly thought that he had been taken at gunpoint by this man, Louis Botha, a very senior Boer commander who later became the first prime minister of the Union of South Africa. His captor was later identified as Sarel Oosthuizen, a unit commander who fought at Colenso and Spion Kop and died of his wounds in 1900.

Churchill was treated as a prisoner of war and taken to Pretoria. Winston and his fellow prisoners were photographed by their captors. He struck a pose on the right and glowered at the cameraman. Churchill claimed that as a reporter, he was a non-combatant. In view of him being in what appeared to be a uniform, armed with a pistol and directing South African troops, the Boers did not believe him. Piet Joubert, the Boer commandant-general, instructed that Churchill must be held for the duration of the war.

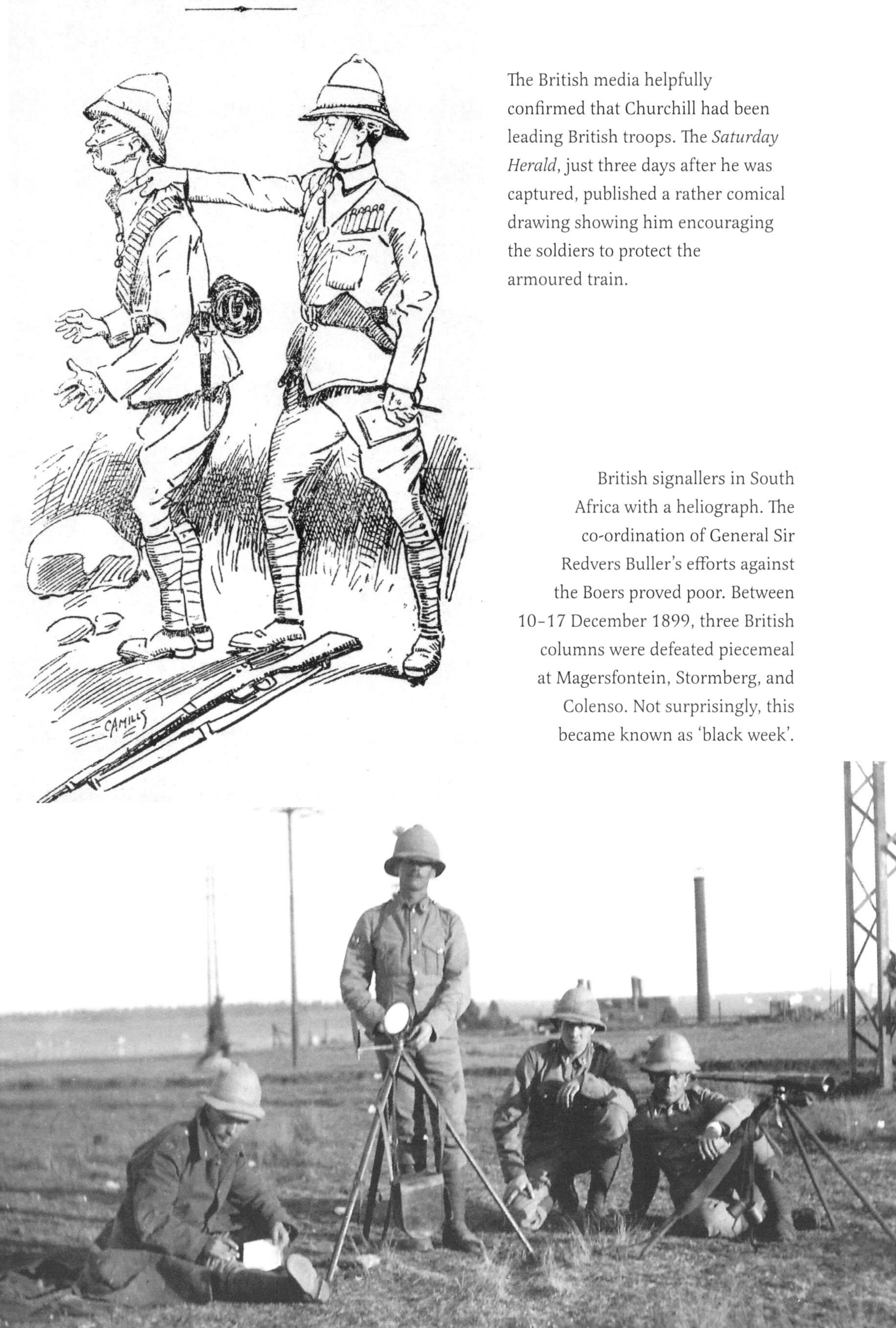

The British media helpfully confirmed that Churchill had been leading British troops. The *Saturday Herald*, just three days after he was captured, published a rather comical drawing showing him encouraging the soldiers to protect the armoured train.

British signallers in South Africa with a heliograph. The co-ordination of General Sir Redvers Buller's efforts against the Boers proved poor. Between 10–17 December 1899, three British columns were defeated piecemeal at Magersfontein, Stormberg, and Colenso. Not surprisingly, this became known as 'black week'.

Field Marshal Lord Roberts was sent to take charge in South Africa, with Lord Kitchener as his chief of staff. General Buller found himself demoted rather than sacked. Roberts was a veteran of the campaigns in India, Abyssinia, and Afghanistan. However, he would not arrive until early January 1900, giving Buller time to make amends on the battlefield and set the British on the road to ultimate victory.

Inadvertently leaving Haldane behind, Churchill escaped from Pretoria on 12 December 1899. The Boers immediately offered a £25 reward for him, dead or alive. The warrant for his capture was wholly unflattering, stating, 'medium build, stooping gait, fair complexion, reddish brown hair, almost invisible slight moustache, speaks through his nose'.

Translation.

£25

(Twenty-five Pounds stg.) REWARD is offered by the Sub-Commission of the fifth division, on behalf of the Special Constable of the said division, to anyone who brings the escaped prisoner of war

CHURCHILL,

dead or alive to this office.

For the Sub-Commission of the fifth division,

(Signed) LODK. de HAAS, Sec.

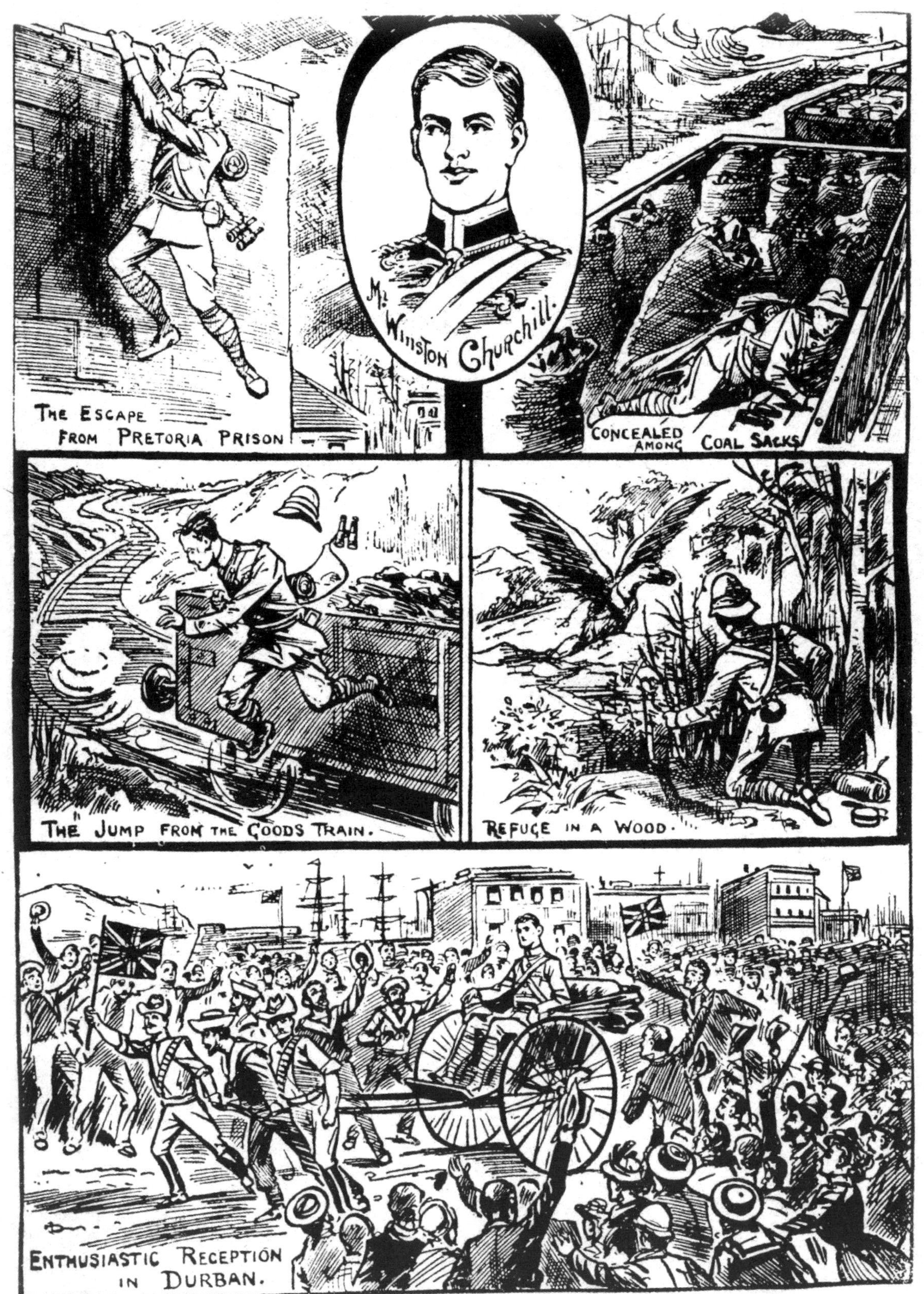

THE ESCAPE OF BRAVE WINSTON CHURCHILL FROM PRETORIA.

SIXTY HOURS OF TERRIBLE ANXIETY AND DARING ADVENTURES

[*Opposite*] Winston's escape became worldwide news, including this graphic depiction of his dramatic exploits by the *Illustrated Police News*. After hiding out at a colliery and jumping several trains, he managed to safely reach Portuguese-controlled Mozambique and sailed to Durban, where he arrived on 23 December 1899 to receive a rapturous hero's welcome.

Afterwards, Churchill revisited the scene of the armoured train's derailment and posed looking decidedly defiant. A wrecked carriage is clearly visible behind him. Once again, he was in bush uniform and armed, note the revolver in the holster beneath his right arm.

Making the most of the photo opportunity, this time mounted. 'Six weeks had passed since the armoured train had been destroyed,' he wrote. 'The hills which I had last seen black with the figures of Boer riflemen were crowned with British pickets.' He also noted that the valley was now covered in British tents.

Churchill stayed in South Africa, securing a lieutenant's commission with the South African Light Horse and continued to work as a journalist. They were known as 'the Sakabulas' because of the black Sakabula bird tail feathers they wore in their slouch hats. When the men were dismounted, this feather was a dangerous lure for snipers, as Churchill was later to discover, almost to his cost. Churchill arranged for his brother Jack to get a commission with the regiment.

The Sakabulas had only been formed in the Cape the previous November. Their ranks included both South Africans and loyalist Afrikaners, as well as, rather surprisingly, a contingent of Texans. Their commander, Lieutenant Colonel Julian 'Bungo' Byng, when he was a captain in the 10th Hussars, first met Churchill in 1894. The South African Light Horse gained the unflattering nickname 'Byng's Burglars' due to their proclivity for stealing. On one embarrassing occasion, Winston recalled, 'The night was chilly. Colonel Byng and I shared a blanket. When he turned over I was in the cold. When I turned over I pulled the blanket off him and he objected. He was the Colonel. It was not a good arrangement.'

Winston was involved in the Battle of Spion Kop on 23 January 1900. When the Lancashire Fusiliers reached what they thought was the summit of the hill, they drove the defending Boers off with a bayonet charge. Ten British soldiers were killed or wounded, while six Boers perished by the bayonet. This, though, was just a taste of things to come. The British had only secured the southern end of the hill, and they came under intense Boer artillery and rifle fire.

Churchill, leaving his unit climbed up to take a look and passed 200 casualties. He was almost shot in the head by a Boer sniper while on the hill; luckily, the round only took off his Sakabula feather. The ground was too hard to dig, and the defenders could only scrape shallow trenches for protection. Eventually, the British, in the face of mounting losses, were forced to withdraw.

The Lancashire Fusiliers, reinforcements from the Imperial Light Infantry, and the Middlesex Regiment suffered 1,200 casualties on Spion Kop. Amongst the dead was Major General Sir Edward Woodgate. These casualties were photographed clogging the main trench, which was barely waist deep.

More British dead in the killing grounds of Spion Kop after the terrible mauling by the Boers. Total British losses during the battle amounted to 243 killed and 1,250 wounded. Despite the heavy casualties, Churchill admired their adversaries. 'They were the most good-hearted enemy,' he later wrote, 'I have ever fought against in the four continents in which it has been my fortune to see Active Service.'

A Boer sniper killed on Spion Kop. It appears he died while trying to reload his rifle. The Boers suffered 68 dead and 267 wounded. 'I have often seen dead men, killed in war — thousands at Omdurman...,' observed Churchill, 'but the Boer dead aroused the most painful emotions.'

Members of the Natal Indian Ambulance Corps, who were sent to look for wounded amongst the dead at Spion Kop. In the second row, third from the right is Mohandas Gandhi, future Indian nationalist leader, whom Churchill would grow to hate when he began to campaign for independence from British rule.

Jack Churchill, standing on the right, photographed by the *Graphic Newspaper* being shipped home from Durban after being wounded. He was commissioned into the Queen's Own Oxfordshire Hussars in 1898, and Winston obtained him a posting with the South African Light Horse. Jack was shot through the leg in February 1900 at the Battle of the Tugela Heights during the operations to relieve Ladysmith. Taken as a souvenir, a piece of the armed train from Chieveley is visible on the deck to the left.

Churchill was next involved in the relief of Ladysmith and then the capture of Pretoria.
On 28 February 1900, he rode into Ladysmith with Major Hubert Gough. 'A poor, white-
faced officer waved his helmet to and fro, and laughed foolishly,' recalled Winston, 'and
the tall, strong colonial horsemen... raised a resounding cheer, for then we knew we had
reached the Ladysmith picket line.' This print shows garrison commander Sir George
White greeting Sir Redvers Buller.

In May 1902, delegates from both sides, including Lord Kitchener, front row, second from the right, got together at Vereeniging, and a peace treaty was signed, ending nearly two years and eight months of war. Under the terms of the agreement, Transvaal and Orange Free State became crown colonies. 'Nearly half a million British and Dominion troops had been employed, of whom one in ten became casualties,' wrote Churchill. 'The total cost in money to the United Kingdom has been reckoned at over two hundred and twenty million pounds.'

Britain lost 21,942 men and the Boers 3,990, though nearly 26,000 died in British concentration camps. Britain agreed to provide £3 million to help with reconstruction. This seemed a paltry sum in light of the amount spent prosecuting the war.

CHAPTER FOUR

A World in Turmoil
1901–1922

Once back home, Churchill succeeded in becoming a Conservative member of parliament. He then defected to join David Lloyd George and the Liberal Party. This gained him his first government job as Under Secretary of State for the Colonies. He then got married and gained his first Cabinet post as President of the Board of Trade. When he was promoted to Home Secretary, his taste for publicity got him into serious trouble, and he was moved to become First Lord of the Admiralty in charge of the Royal Navy. During the First World War, he was forced to resign over his Gallipoli campaign, and he went for a while to the Western Front as a battalion commander. Afterwards, Churchill was back in government as the Minister of Munitions. After the conflict ended, he became Secretary of State for War and Air, then Secretary of State for the Colonies. Both posts constantly thrust him into the international limelight.

Winston wasted no time in
relaunching his political career.
Just five days after getting back
from South Africa, he was once
more adopted as the Conservative
candidate for Oldham on 25
July 1900. He won the seat on 1
October that year, just two months
short of his twenty-sixth birthday.
Instead of attending the opening of
Parliament the following month, he
embarked on a lucrative speaking
tour of Britain, the United States,
and Canada. In light of him
inheriting almost no money and
MPs at the time being unpaid, he
had little choice but to capitalise
on his adventures and writing. He
finally took his seat in Parliament
in February 1901. When he made
his maiden speech, it was to attack
his own party's proposal to increase
defence spending. He also wrote
two books about his time in South
Africa, *London to Ladysmith* and *Ian
Hamilton's March*.

Churchill crossed the floor of the
House of Commons in 1904 to join
David Lloyd George on the Liberal
benches after disagreeing with
Prime Minister Arthur Balfour's
policy of protectionism and moves
to curb Jewish immigration. Lloyd
George would become a mentor
to Churchill, especially when it
came to welfare reform. Sadly, their
relationship would sour during
the Second World War.

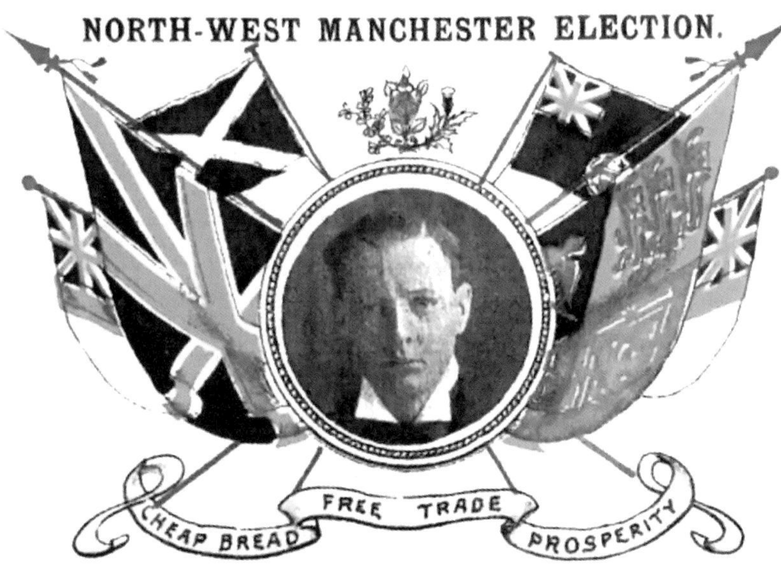

After his defection, Churchill was deselected by his Conservative constituency in Oldham. In the 1906 General Election, he championed the Manchester North West parliamentary seat for the Liberals and notably, on his election literature, as a free trade candidate. He won and was back in Parliament.

In Henry Campbell-Bannerman's Liberal government, Churchill was appointed Under Secretary of State for the Colonies. He inevitably came to the attention of Campbell-Bannerman because the Foreign Secretary, Lord Elgin, was a member of the House of Lords. This meant that Churchill regularly spoke for his department in the House of Commons. His time at the Colonial Office inevitably helped shape his views on the British Empire and, in particular, India. The following year, he was sworn in as a Privy Councillor and spent four months visiting Kenya, Uganda, and Sudan. This resulted in another book called *My African Journey*.

Churchill with Kaiser Wilhelm II in 1906 during
Imperial German Army manoeuvres in Breslau.
Winston noted, 'All he wished was to feel like
Napoleon'. Campbell-Bannerman cautioned the
outspoken Churchill not to cause a diplomatic
incident by speaking too candidly with the Kaiser.
Winston must have made a good impression, as
he was invited back to Germany three years later.
The militaristic Kaiser was destined to lead his
country into a terrible world war.

In 1908, Winston became engaged to Miss
Clementine Hozier. They married at St
Margaret's Church, Westminster, London, on
Saturday, 12 September that year. Appropriately, the
location was the parish church of the House of Commons.
The service was conducted by the Bishop of St Asaph. Giving
the address, the Dean of Manchester, Bishop James Welldon,
Winston's former headmaster at Harrow, astutely said, 'The
influence which the wives of our statesmen have exercised
for good upon their husbands' lives is an unwritten chapter
of English history, too sacred perhaps to be written in full.'
He then concluded, 'May your lives prove a blessing, each to the
other, and both to the world.' They did not disappoint him.

[*Opposite*] Their wedding was treated as a major society event by the newspapers,
with it making the front pages of a number of publications such as *The Daily
Graphic*, *Daily Mirror*, and *Evening News*. In America, *The New York Times* covered it.
Madame Tussaud's on the wedding day placed a life-sized model of the bridegroom
on public display. The *Tailor and Cutter* trade journal was scathing about Winston's
outfit, writing, 'one of the greatest failures as a wedding garment we have ever
seen, giving the wearer a sort of glorified coachman appearance.'

No. 5852.—Vol. LXXV.

THE DAILY GRAPHIC

ONE PENNY

LONDON: MONDAY, SEPTEMBER 14, 1908.

REGISTERED AS A NEWSPAPER.

THE MARRIAGE OF A CABINET MINISTER.

THE BRIDESMAIDS.

MR. CHURCHILL AND HIS BRIDE PASSING DOWN THE NAVE AFTER THE MARRIAGE CEREMONY.

THE BRIDEGROOM ARRIVES AT THE CHURCH.
("Daily Graphic" Photograph.)

THE CHURCHILL-HOZIER WEDDING AT ST. MARGARET'S, WESTMINSTER, ON SATURDAY AFTERNOON.   (See page 3.)

Mr and Mrs Churchill. Winston's best man, Lord Hugh Cecil, observed, 'Marriage will be excellent for you mentally, morally and politically. A bachelor is regarded as morally unprincipled.' The newlyweds spent their honeymoon at Blenheim Palace and in Italy. From Blenheim, he wrote to his mother and betrayed some understandable groom's nerves, 'What a relief to have got that ceremony over! & so happily.'

The happy couple step out to be greeted by the press. Clementine's look of contentment speaks volumes for the strength of their relationship. Winston wrote, 'I married and lived happily ever afterwards.' Also in 1908, at the age of thirty-three, he replaced Lloyd George as President of the Board of Trade and entered the Cabinet. His political star was rising. Lloyd George, in turn, became Chancellor of the Exchequer. In his new role, Churchill was determined to push through welfare reforms and instigate what he called the 'Minimum Standard.'

Lloyd George's proposed People's Budget, with its increased social welfare programmes, met stiff opposition from the House of Lords, which invoked its veto. This sparked a general election in early 1910, and *Punch* magazine showed Churchill and Lloyd George celebrating the news. The Liberals won, and the Lords, branded unconstitutional, were silenced.

Winston was appointed Home Secretary in 1910 by Herbert Henry Asquith, the new prime minister who had replaced an ailing Campbell-Bannerman. Lloyd George and Churchill on their way to the House of Commons for the Chancellor's controversial budget on 27 April 1910. Churchill wrote to Asquith, stating, 'The time has come for the total abolition of the House of Lords.' The budget was passed by the Commons and the Lords did not oppose it.

Winston was soon courting controversy in the role of Home Secretary when he attended the siege of 100 Sidney Street on 3 January 1911. There, two armed Latvian anarchists, who the previous December had killed three police officers in the course of a jewellery robbery, were cornered by the police. Winston, at the time, was in his bath at home in Eccleston Square, Pimlico, but rather than asking to be kept informed, quickly rushed to the scene. When members of the Scots Guards arrived, the situation escalated and there was much shooting.

Churchill, foolishly attending the incident personally, ordered the police and fire brigade to hold back. He told Asquith, 'I thought it better to let the house burn down, than spend good British lives in rescuing those ferocious rascals.' His greatest concern was to avoid being shot in the backside by the armed police officer behind him. The Latvians perished in the house. To make matters worse, the siege had been filmed by *Pathé News*. The following day, the newspapers were outraged by the Home Secretary's heavy-handed conduct. An inquest was held, and Churchill maintained, 'I never directed anyone to send for a Maxim [machine] gun, nor did I send at any time for further military force.' Churchill had arrived to find the army already there.

In October 1911, Churchill was moved from the Home Office and made First Lord of the Admiralty. This role required him to implement the reforms of Admiral 'Jacky' Fisher, the First Sea Lord, seen here on the left, who had retired earlier in the year. At the Admiralty, Winston oversaw the dreadnought battleship programme, built up the Royal Navy Air Service and introduced a naval staff for the very first time. He also developed a taste for flying until Clementine prevailed upon him to stop before he killed himself.

Churchill and Clementine about to enjoy a trip on board the Admiralty yacht HMS *Enchantress*. Churchill first visited the 4,000-tonne vessel on 5 November 1911 at Cowes, Isle of Wight, from where he sailed to Portsmouth naval base. The following year, he wrote, 'I have carefully considered the general question of the Admiralty yacht, and have come to the conclusion that it should be retained. It is desirable, in the public interest, that the visits of the Board of Admiralty to the ports and to the fleets should be frequent, and that members of the Board, particularly the First Lord himself as the Parliamentary head, should have opportunities of seeing things with their own eyes, and of getting to know and keeping in touch with officers in the dock yards and the seagoing fleets.' In other words, he had no intention of giving it up.

Churchill, in his First Lord of the Admiralty sailing attire. He used the *Enchantress* to visit numerous British warships and naval bases around Britain and in the Mediterranean. While he utilised the yacht as a floating office, not surprisingly, he used it, particularly in the Mediterranean, for pleasure trips and sightseeing. Before the outbreak of the First World War, he spent a total of eight months on the vessel. This led to questions in the House of Commons. Churchill was later to confess, 'It was the finest toy I ever had in my life.'

DOGG'D.

Winston. " *Ship's* biscuit, I think." [May 29, 1912.]

The bulldog seeing off the terrier. This was how *Punch* magazine saw Churchill in his role of First Lord of the Admiralty in 1912, fending off Lloyd George's attempts to reallocate unspent funding. The start of the First World War in the summer of 1914 proved an embarrassment for Churchill and the Admiralty. German U-boats neutralised his Grand Fleet, and German cruisers reached Constantinople, resulting in the Ottoman Empire siding with Germany. Admiral Fisher was recalled from retirement to serve as First Sea Lord for a second time.

Upon the outbreak of war, Churchill was dubbed one of the 'Men of the Moment'. This postcard proclaimed reassuringly, 'Aye Ready!' Another stated 'Rt. Hon. Winston Churchill, As one who hitherto has won Our complete confidence — We Britons — in this crisis — trust the "power behind the fleet."' It would not be long before Churchill lost public confidence thanks to his overly ambitious strategic designs.

Churchill sent the Royal Navy Division, comprising a brigade of Royal Marines and two brigades of sailors fighting as infantry, to Antwerp to help with its defence. He travelled to the port on 3 October 1914 with the aim of commanding the garrison. Prime Minister Asquith immediately ordered him home, and Antwerp fell to the Germans seven days later.

Churchill next advocated an assault on the Dardanelles, the narrow entrance to the Black Sea. He reasoned that by capturing Constantinople, it would knock the Ottoman Empire out of the war and take the pressure off the Western and Eastern Fronts. In principle, this was a sound plan if executed properly; however, the Royal Navy and the British Army were to bungle things from the very start.

The British and French fleets began shelling the Turkish outer forts in the Dardanelles in early November 1914, thereby alerting the Turkish government that an attack was imminent. The landings did not take place at Cape Helles and further north at what was dubbed ANZAC (Australian and New Zealand Army Corps) Cove until 25 April 1915. These were easily contained by the Turkish army, which had been trained by the Germans. The Allies proved unable to break out of their two bridgeheads.

The inspiration for the tank — the American Holt 75 model gasoline-powered caterpillar tractor. It was deployed by both the British and French armies to tow artillery on the Western Front. The prominent front tiller wheel was discontinued on the later models. War correspondent Lieutenant Colonel Ernest Swinton, while driving through France, in October 1914, first came up with the idea of a tracked armoured fighting vehicle to help break the deadlock of trench warfare on the Western Front.

Lieutenant Colonel Swinton's proposal for a tracked combat vehicle landed on Churchill's desk at the Admiralty in January 1915 as the Royal Navy was operating armoured cars in France. Swinton was inspired by reports of the Holt caterpillar tractor after an engineering friend had seen one in action in Antwerp. Churchill liked the idea and took it to Asquith, and set up the Landship Committee.

The Number I Lincoln Machine prototype built by William Foster and Company made its first test run in September 1915. Problems with its tracks led to 'Little Willie' and ultimately the British Mark I-V tank. Asquith instructed Lloyd George's Ministry of Munitions and the Royal Navy's Landships Committee to merge their efforts as the Tank Supply Committee. To hide its true purpose, the hull was designated a water carrier or water tank destined for Mesopotamia. Swinton suggested that the term 'tank' be kept as the vehicle's permanent name.

In mid-May 1915, Admiral Fisher resigned as First Sea Lord, signalling a lack of faith in Churchill's leadership. This forced Winston to step down from his position at the Admiralty. 'I am finished,' he wrote despondently to newspaper proprietor Lord Riddell. The latter, who was a supporter of Lloyd George, showed little sympathy for Churchill's plight. The Dardanelles stalemate rumbled on until the ANZACs were evacuated in December 1915 and Helles Bay was evacuated in January 1916. The fruitless eight-month Gallipoli campaign was a costly political and military failure for which Churchill was unfairly held responsible.

A despondent Churchill, following his humiliating resignation from the Admiralty, volunteered for service on the Western Front. Lord Kitchener, seeking to console Churchill, said, 'There is one thing at any rate they cannot take from you: the Fleet was ready.' Promoted to Lieutenant Colonel, he was appointed commander of the 6th Battalion, Royal Scots Fusiliers. His second in command was Major Archibald Sinclair, the future leader of the Liberal Party and Secretary of State for Air, seated to the left. Churchill remained on the Western Front until May 1916, when he returned to London to resume his seat in the House of Commons.

Churchill liked to take the credit for the invention of the tank, but it was Lloyd George, firstly as Minister of Munitions, subsequently Secretary of State for War, then Prime Minister, who proved to be the most ardent supporter of the concept. It was he who, while still Minister of Munitions, authorised production of the tank. In July 1917, six months after Lloyd George became Prime Minister, he made Churchill the Minister of Munitions. As a result, all the praise was heaped on Churchill. John Oborne with the 4th Battalion, Devonshire Regiment, was very grateful, noting, 'You had a certain amount of shielding because you used to follow the tanks along. They were a great help. They'd flatten the wire. I know they were in their infancy, but Churchill did a good job with them.' Crucially, the tank did help end the war. Despondent German soldiers called it 'Germany's Downfall'.

British troops gassed by German phosgene. Gas warfare was another aspect of the First World War that Churchill was involved in. When he became Minister of Munitions, he was responsible for the manufacture of chemical weapons. However, it should be pointed out that he was in no way responsible for their deployment, which first happened two years before his appointment when Germany unleashed chlorine, followed by mustard and phosgene gas on the battlefield. The Allies then retaliated. Churchill's factories produced 100 tonnes of mustard gas, which were deployed in September 1918. He wrote rather glibly to Clementine, 'The hamper of mustard gas is on its way.' Churchill always felt that mustard gas was actually a more humane weapon, on the basis that it killed less than 10 per cent of its victims. Privately, though, he acknowledged that it was a 'hellish poison'. Subsequently the use of chemical weapons was banned internationally in 1925 under the Geneva Protocol.

Churchill in Lille on 29 October 1918, watching a liberation parade just before the end of the First World War. That day Clementine wrote to him saying, 'I would like you to be praised as a reconstructive genius as well as a Mustard Gas Fiend, a Tank juggernaut and a flying Terror... Can't the men Munition Workers build lovely garden cities?' Two days later, Turkey surrendered, followed by the Austro-Hungarian Empire. Germany finally capitulated on 11 November 1918.

Churchill, serving as Secretary of State for War and Air, smoking outside the House of Commons with Edward, Prince of Wales, on 5 June 1919. They first met at the Prince's investiture in 1911. Two years later, Churchill wrote to Clementine about Edward, 'He is so nice, and we have made rather friends. They are worried a little about him, ... He requires to fall in love with a pretty cat.' This, though, would prove extremely problematic.

In his role as Secretary of State for War, on 19 August 1919, Churchill reviewed the troops of the British Army of Occupation in Cologne. A formal parade was held for him in Cathedral Square. This was part of an Allied force tasked with occupying the German Rhineland under the terms of the First World War Armistice and subsequent Treaty of Versailles. The Rhineland would remain demilitarized until 1936, when Adolf Hitler marched back in.

Churchill, as Secretary of State for the Colonies, in March 1921, during the Cairo
Conference, oversaw the dismemberment of the vanquished Ottoman Empire. This led
to the creation of Iraq and Transjordan. He also confirmed Britain's commitment to
a Jewish national home in Palestine. Two of his advisers were Colonel T.E. Lawrence,
better known as 'Lawrence of Arabia' and Gertrude Bell, the 'Queen of the Desert'. Bell
was the only woman amongst the forty conference delegates. Clementine Churchill
is standing on the right, while fourth from the right is Emir Abdullah of Transjordan.
Churchill also visited the British Mandate of Palestine, which encompassed modern-day
Gaza, Israel, Jordan, and the West Bank, all previously part of the Ottoman Empire.

During the Russian Civil War, Churchill supported the pro-Tsarist forces of Admiral
Alexander Kolchak, seated, against the revolutionary Bolsheviks. However, by October
1922, they had been soundly defeated by the vastly better coordinated Red Army.
Joseph Stalin, who became General Secretary of the Communist Party that year, never
forgave the West for its intervention in Russia's domestic affairs and its attempts to
strangle Bolshevism at birth.

Wilderness Years

1923-1939

During the 1920s, Churchill rejoined the Conservative Party and became Chancellor of the Exchequer. Subsequent Labour and coalition governments throughout the 1930s, coupled with his opposition to self-government for India, ensured Churchill was excluded from Cabinet roles. He spent his time warning about the perils of German rearmament and opposing Prime Minister Neville Chamberlain's policy of appeasement towards Adolf Hitler. Churchill was not a lone anti-appeaser, but he was seen as their very vocal figurehead. It was not until Hitler invaded Poland in 1939 that Churchill was finally invited back into government by Chamberlain as First Lord of the Admiralty.

When Stanley Baldwin led the Conservatives to victory in 1924, defeating Ramsay MacDonald's short-lived Labour government, he appointed Churchill, who had rejoined them as Chancellor of the Exchequer. 'I was surprised,' said Winston, 'and the Conservative Party dumbfounded when he (Mr Baldwin) invited me to become Chancellor of the Exchequer, the office which my father once held.'

Churchill was confronted by deflation after returning the country to the gold standard, which fuelled wage reductions and stifled exports. This understandably proved very damaging to his Chancellorship and to the Conservatives. Economic strife sparked the nine-day General Strike in 1926. During which Churchill drew on his journalist skills to edit and write eight editions of the government-funded *British Gazette* newspaper. He continued to serve in his role as Chancellor of the Exchequer until June 1929, when the Conservatives lost the General Election to Labour.

The British Gazette

Published by His Majesty's Stationery Office.

No. 2.   LONDON, THURSDAY, MAY 6, 1926.   ONE PENNY

NATION CALM AND CONFIDENT

Gradual Recommencement of the Railway Services.

GOOD FUEL AND FOOD SUPPLIES.

Volunteers In Large Numbers At All The Centres.

FOREIGN VIEWS OF THE STRIKE.

Liberty and the State.

THE WAY OF FASCISM.

"ORGANISED MENACE."

The Real Issue Behind the General Strike.

But Door Still Open.

T.U.C. FLOUTED

Hospital without Electricity.

WORK DISORGANISED.

Operating Theatres Closed.

MESSAGE FROM THE PRIME MINISTER

Constitutional Government is being attacked.

Let all good citizens whose livelihood and labour have thus been put in peril bear with fortitude and patience the hardships with which they have been suddenly confronted. Stand behind the Government, who are doing their part, confident that you will co-operate in the measures they have undertaken to preserve the liberties and privileges of the people of these islands. The laws of England are the people's birthright. The laws are in your keeping. You have made Parliament their guardian. The General Strike is a challenge to Parliament and is the road to anarchy and ruin.

STANLEY BALDWIN.

From 1929 to 1931, Labour was back
in power under Ramsay MacDonald.
He would then head a national or
coalition government from 1931 to
1935. Churchill dubbed MacDonald
'the Boneless Wonder'. One of
MacDonald's first moves was to
negotiate the London Naval Treaty
seeking reductions amongst the fleets
of Britain, France, Italy, Japan, and
the United States. 'If you wish for
disarmament, it will be necessary to
go to the political and economic causes
which lie behind the maintenance of
armies and navies,' warned Churchill.

Winston, while on tour in
America in 1929, met the
movie star Charlie Chaplin.
When Chaplin visited
England two years later, he
noted of Churchill's home,
'Chartwell is a lovely old
house, modestly furnished,
but in good taste, with a
family feeling about it.' To
Churchill's displeasure,
Chaplin, who supported
Indian independence, then
met with Mahatma Gandhi.

The Hindu-dominated Indian National Congress, led by Mahatma Gandhi and
Jawaharlal Nehru, in late 1929, declared self-rule in defiance of the British Raj. Gandhi,
in early 1930, led the twenty-four-day Salt March as an act of civil disobedience against
the British salt monopoly. This led to widespread protests across India in support, and
about 60,000 people were arrested. Churchill joined the newly formed India Empire
Society that campaigned against constitutional reform for India. In January 1931, he
resigned from the Shadow Cabinet in protest over plans to give some self-government
to India. Churchill's opposition to granting India dominion status ensured that from
1931-39 he was given no opposition or government posts. He dubbed this period his
'wilderness years'. Although he held no ministerial roles, he was active in opposing the
government's weak response to German and Italian militarism. Churchill claimed, 'I
can truthfully affirm that I never felt resentment, still less pain at being so decisively
discarded in a moment of national stress.'

Gandhi arriving in the East End of London on 22 September 1931 to meet Charlie Chaplin. He came to London for the Second Round Table Conference to discuss constitutional reforms in India. Gandhi and other Congress leaders had been freed from prison after the failure of the First Round. Sir Samuel Hoare, the newly appointed Secretary of State for India, committed to self-government for India, but Gandhi would settle for nothing less than full independence. The conference led to the Government of India Act 1935.

Sir Samuel Hoare was one of Churchill's key political opponents during the 'wilderness years'. Hoare, an ardent anti-Bolshevist, was worried about the influence of the Indian Communist Party, and favoured Gandhi and the Congress Party. Churchill did everything he could to oppose and delay the introduction of Hoare's Government of India Act 1935, that increased the Indian electorate and introduced autonomy for the provinces and the concept of a federation of India. Churchill sought to discredit Hoare by accusing him of breaching parliamentary privilege, which further soured their relationship.

Churchill disliked Gandhi immensely for fear that Indian independence would spell the end of the British Empire and partition for the Raj. 'Jailing him would be a very simple solution if it would work,' Chaplain cautioned Churchill, 'but if you imprison one Gandhi, another will arise.' Churchill claimed, 'Gandhi stands for the permanent exclusion of British trade from India. Gandhi stands for the substitution of Brahmin domination for British rule in India. You will never be able to come to terms with Gandhi.'

Churchill's other preoccupation during the early 1930s was the rise to power of Adolf
Hitler in Germany. Hitler, on 30 January 1933, became Chancellor of the German
Reich. On 14 October, he withdrew from the re-convened disarmament conference and
a week later left the League of Nations. Churchill, in his correspondence to Clementine,
began referring to Hitler as 'that gangster'. The following year, Hitler became the
president of Nazi Germany. Churchill was increasingly alarmed by the rate of Nazi
rearmament. 'I dread the day when the means of threatening the heart of the British
Empire should pass into the hands of the present rulers of Germany,' Winston told the
House of Commons on 8 March 1934.

Traffic jam on Westminster Bridge in London in 1935 with the Houses of Parliament shrouded in scaffolding and fog. Britain's coalition government remained in denial about Hitler's rapid preparations for war. In the summer that year, Prime Minister Ramsay MacDonald resigned and was replaced by Stanley Baldwin. 'He was largely detached from foreign and military affairs,' observed Winston of the latter. 'He knew little of Europe and disliked what he knew.'

French workers laying the groundwork for France's defences. Through the 1930s, France embarked on a massive programme to create the concrete fortifications of the Maginot Line facing the German border. This was considered the jewel in the crown of the country's defensive measures that sought to emulate the stronghold of Verdun, which had held out against the Germans during the First World War. In a stroke, France passed the military initiative over to Germany in any future war by tying her forces to fixed defences.

First World War vintage French Renault FT-17 light tanks on parade in Paris in the mid-1930s. It was not until late 1938 that the French War Council decided to equip two armoured divisions on the Charles de Gaulle pattern. By then, it was far too late; the Germans could muster twelve hard-hitting panzer divisions. Although France had one of the most powerful and best-equipped armies in Europe, the French government lacked the political will to use it or formulate a coherent strategy.

In 1936, Hitler sent his troops into the demilitarised Rhineland in violation of the Treaty of Versailles, but Britain and France did nothing in response. Prime Minister Stanley Baldwin, leading a coalition government, argued that Britain was not in a position to oppose this. Churchill warned the House of Commons, 'Europe is approaching a climax. I believe that climax will be reached in the lifetime of the present Parliament.' That year, he travelled to Paris to give a speech with the hope of galvanising French opposition to Nazi Germany.

A BAND OF HOPE.

(*Left to right :* Sir A. CH——N, Lord W———N, Sir R——T H——NE, Mr. W——N CH——LL.)

"WE DREAMT THAT WE DWELT IN MARBLE HALLS . . ."

'A Band of Hope' was published by *Punch* on 3 June 1936. It showed, left to right, Austen Chamberlain, Lord Winterton, Sir Robert Horne, and Churchill. At the time, all four, despite being excluded from government, were urging the country to look to its defences or face the consequences. Hence the pun 'The "Shadow" Music Cabinet'.

Churchill got himself into trouble when he supported King Edward VIII's wish to marry his twice-divorced American mistress, Wallis Simpson. His friendship with the king since before the First World War, when Edward was still the Prince of Wales, had flourished. This brought Churchill into conflict with Prime Minister Baldwin, whose government did not approve of a union that would see Simpson become queen. Baldwin wanted the king to end the relationship, but he refused, sparking the Abdication Crisis in December 1936.

Edward VIII stepped down in order to marry Simpson, with them going into exile as the Duke and Duchess of Windsor. He was succeeded by his brother Albert, who became George VI on 12 May 1937. Initially, George VI, who had never anticipated being king, was understandably displeased by Churchill's support for his brother. Baldwin saw Churchill's position as a power play against him, and Winston was left discredited and isolated in the House of Commons. Baldwin, though, stepped down and was replaced by fellow Conservative, Neville Chamberlain.

In 1937, Japanese troops overran Shanghai, which threatened Western interests in the city. 'China, as the years pass,' wrote Churchill that September, 'is being eaten by Japan like an artichoke, leaf by leaf.' The Japanese had been waging war on the Chinese since the early 1930s and by this stage had 700,000 troops in China. 'I must admit that, having voted for the Japanese alliance nearly forty years ago and having always done my very best to promote good relations with the Island Empire of Japan,' said Churchill, 'and always having been a sentimental well-wisher to the Japanese ... I should view [war with them] with keen sorrow.'

When the Japanese stormed into Nanking in late 1937, they massacred up to 300,000 Chinese civilians in an orgy of violence. Churchill's pro-Japan stance looked ill-advised, and he ignored what had happened. 'If the Chinese now suffer the cruel malice and oppression of their enemies,' he wrote, 'it is the fault of the base and perverted conception of pacificism their rulers have ingrained for two or three thousand years on their people.' This was not true; the Chinese were fighting for their lives, but were outmatched by the superior Japanese military. American author Iris Chang subsequently criticised Western histories for overlooking what happened in Nanking, in particular noting, 'Nor can a word of the massacre be found in Winston Churchill's famous Memoirs of the Second World War.' At the time, Churchill did not want to face up to the prospect of war with Japan when war was looming in Europe.

Foreign Secretary Anthony Eden resigned on 20 February 1938 in protest at Prime Minister Chamberlain's policy of friendship toward Benito Mussolini's Fascist Italy. Following Italy's brutal conquest of Abyssinia (Ethiopia) intelligence showed that Mussolini posed a threat to British interests in the Mediterranean. Eden would serve again as Foreign Secretary under Churchill during the Second World War and in the 1950s.

Churchill watched in dismay in March 1938 when Hitler marched into Austria declaring an Anschluss or union with Germany. In response Churchill told the House of Commons, 'Europe is confronted with a programme of aggression, nicely calculated and timed, unfolding stage by stage, and there is only one choice open, not only to us, but to other countries... either submit, like Austria, or else take effective measures while time remains'. The Austrians did not resist the annexation of their country and Nazi Germany became stronger than ever. 'Thus by every device, from stick to the carrot,' wrote Churchill, 'the emaciated Austrian donkey is made to pull the Nazi barrow up an ever-steepening hill.'

Chamberlain and his coalition government felt that appeasing Hitler was a better option than costly rearmament and another war in Europe. Churchill was unconvinced that Hitler would be satisfied by Chamberlain's foolhardy Munich agreement in September 1938. This let Hitler annex the German speaking Sudetenland from Czechoslovakia leaving the rest of the weakened country to its fate. 'We are in the presence of a disaster of the first magnitude,' he told the House of Commons on 5 October 1938. The Czech and Slovak lands split, with Hitler occupying the former the following year. 'The Czech lands have been plundered,' said Churchill, ''and every scrap of food and useful portable article carried off to Germany by organised brigandage or common theft.' In particular Hitler got his hands on Skoda's sizeable weapons factories that were producing small arms, artillery and tanks.

Churchill's time in the political wilderness came to a dramatic end. Adolf Hitler's Blitzkrieg, or Lightning War, rolled into Poland at 0445 hours on 1 September 1939. That same day the Luftwaffe's bombers hit the Polish capital Warsaw. Britain and France as allies of Poland were obliged to declare war on Germany just two days later. 'Honour was the sole reason why we had drawn the sword to help Poland against Hitler's brutal onslaught,' said Churchill. Much to his delight the British Dominions swiftly came to Britain's help. Australia and New Zealand at that point also declared war on Germany.

Winston, just after Hitler invaded Poland, was invited back into government as First Lord of the Admiralty. On 4 September 1939 he stood on the steps outside the Admiralty and had this iconic photo taken. 'No one had ever been over the same course twice with such an interval between...,' remarked Churchill. 'I could feel that I had effectively taken over the great Department which I knew so well and loved with a discriminating eye... I certainly felt prepared to discharge that duty in fact as well as form.' His first tests would be in the Atlantic and Norway.

Jan Smuts, whom Churchill had known since the Boer War, became prime minister of South Africa a second time on 5 September 1939. Although some South African politicians wanted their country to remain neutral, the following day, Smuts declared war on Germany and the Axis. He would prove to be a valued close friend and confidant of Churchill's during the war, such was his competence. It was even suggested that after Churchill became prime minister, he should be nominated as Churchill's successor.

In a show of solidarity, Canadian Prime Minister William Lyon Mackenzie King declared war on Germany on 10 September 1939. From a standing start, the expansion of Canada's armed forces would be rapid and dramatic. He promised that only volunteers would serve overseas; unfortunately, this would eventually put incredible strain on the Canadian Army.

Chamberlain's War Cabinet. Standing left to right: Sir John Anderson, Minister for Home Security; Lord Maurice Hankey, Minister without Portfolio; Leslie Hoare Belisha, Secretary of State for War; Winston Churchill, First Lord of the Admiralty; Sir Kingsley Wood, Air Minister; Anthony Eden, Secretary of State for Dominion Affairs; Sir Edward Bridges, Permanent Secretary and Secretary of the War Cabinet. Front row left to right: Lord Halifax, Foreign Secretary; Sir John Simon, Chancellor of the Exchequer; Neville Chamberlain, Prime Minister; Sir Samuel Hoare, Lord Privy Seal; Lord Ernle Chatfield, Minister for the Co-ordination of Defence.

British and French soldiers photographed during the winter Phoney War of 1939-40. The British Army committed over a dozen divisions to the defence of northern France, supported by an armoured brigade and an armoured division. Within four months of this photo being taken, these men would find themselves on the receiving end of Hitler's Blitzkrieg. First, though, on 9 April 1940, Hitler invaded Denmark and Norway.

CHAPTER SIX

Finest Hour

1940

In May 1940, Hitler invaded much of western Europe and a humiliated Chamberlain was forced to resign. Churchill found himself invited to head a coalition government. He rapidly faced a growing crisis over the fate of the British Expeditionary Force trapped at Dunkirk and then the Luftwaffe assaulting the British Isles. Authorising the successful evacuation of the BEF and his firm resolve during the Battle of Britain and the Blitz proved to be his finest hour. During this time, Churchill very much made himself the public figure of Britain's opposition to Hitler's occupation of the Continent. He knew, though, that Britain could not win the war on its own.

Prime Minister Neville Chamberlain, with
German troops in Denmark and Norway,
faced a very hostile House of Commons
on 7 May 1940. Lloyd George, gunning
for him, accused Britain's intervention
in Norway of being 'half-baked'.
Churchill took full responsibility as
First Lord of the Admiralty, but Lloyd
George would not be deterred, saying
'the right honourable gentleman must
not allow himself to be converted into
an air-raid shelter to keep the splinters
from hitting his colleagues.' Many
MPs from all the political parties felt
Chamberlain should step down, and the
beleaguered prime minister only just survived
a vote of no confidence.

Within Conservative circles, Edward
Wood, Lord Halifax, the Foreign
Secretary, was the preferred successor
for Chamberlain, but as a member
of the House of Lords, he technically
could not become prime minister in
the House of Commons. Furthermore,
as one of the key architects of the
government's policy of appeasement
towards Hitler, he was tainted. In
some quarters, it was thought he
lacked drive. Churchill, despite
being a well-qualified contender, was
considered too old and too much
of a wild card. Although he was
popular with the Labour and Liberal
parties, thanks to his opposition to
appeasement, he was not popular with
many Conservatives. Nonetheless,
Churchill soon became the favourite
as Halifax did not want the job.

Churchill crossing Horse Guards Parade, London. On 10 May 1940, Hitler invaded the Low Countries, Luxembourg, and France. Chamberlain resigned, and Churchill was summoned by King George VI and asked to form a new coalition government. Churchill needed Chamberlain's support as he remained leader of the Conservative Party, so ensured that he and Halifax were initially in his War Cabinet. Churchill soon moved into 10 Downing Street in London, the traditional residence of the British prime minister.

Clement Attlee, leader of the Labour Party, joined Churchill's Cabinet as Lord Privy Seal (essentially a minister without portfolio). He would become Britain's first-ever deputy prime minister in February 1942. Attlee was a veteran of the Gallipoli campaign, which he supported and felt could have been a success if it had been carried out properly. This made him a supporter of Churchill as a military strategist. Attlee and Churchill agreed that the War Cabinet should comprise three Conservatives, initially Churchill, Chamberlain and Halifax and two Labour members, initially Attlee and Arthur Greenwood. They also agreed that Labour should have slightly more than one-third of the ministerial posts in the coalition government.

Members of Churchill's Coalition Cabinet in May 1940. Left to right, front row: Sir John Anderson Home Secretary and Minister of Home Security, Churchill, Attlee, Anthony Eden Secretary of State for War then Secretary of State for Foreign Affairs; back row: Sir Stafford Cripps Ambassador to the Soviet Union then Lord Privy Seal, Ernest Bevin Minister of Labour and National Service, Lord Beaverbrook Minister of Aircraft Production then Minister of Supply and Minister of War Production and Herbert Morrison Minister of Supply then Home Secretary.

Issued by the Ministry of Information, this rousing propaganda poster, displaying a determined-looking Churchill and British military might, was intended to signal a firm end to Chamberlain's appeasement. It was inspired by Winston's first speech as prime minister to the House of Commons on 13 May 1940, in which he famously said, 'I have nothing to offer but blood, toil, tears and sweat' and concluded with, 'Come then, let us go forward together with our united strength.'

The very day that Churchill made his inaugural speech to the Commons, the German 1st, 2nd and 10th Panzer Divisions attacked across the river Meuse at Sedan. The tanks of General Erwin Rommel's 7th Panzer Division also crossed to the north at Dinant the next day. French efforts to halt them getting over the river failed, despite three of the seven crossings being stopped; the others succeeded. In addition, the Luftwaffe quickly gained control of the skies, its bombs sowing panic on the roads and railways.

French prisoners of war being led off into captivity. The two French divisions holding the river soon collapsed. The French 55th Infantry Division, which bore the brunt of the attack at Sedan, was well equipped with artillery but lacked training and anti-tank guns. The German breakthrough enabled the panzers to race westward toward the English Channel. This left the British Expeditionary Force and the French army that had advanced into Belgium terribly exposed.

Fearing invasion, Churchill first called for the creation of a home guard in October 1939, recruiting men over the age of 40. With the cream of the British Army on the Continent on 14 May 1940, the formation of the Local Defence Volunteers was announced by Anthony Eden, Secretary of State for War. Uncharitably dubbed 'Dad's Army', they initially lacked training and were extremely poorly equipped.

That same day, the Luftwaffe, in an overwhelming show of strength, bombed Rotterdam, killing 800 people and destroying 25,000 homes, leaving some 78,000 people homeless. The stunned Dutch government was forced to surrender. Churchill knew that it would not be long before Britain's cities received similar treatment if he did not yield.

An anxious Churchill, deeply concerned by a growing sense of French defeatism, flew to meet the French premier Paul Reynaud on 16 May 1940. Reynaud wanted the Royal Air Force to commit more of its fighter squadrons to France, which would endanger Britain's air defence. Four days later, Hitler's panzers reached the English Channel at Abbeville, cutting off Boulogne, Calais, and Dunkirk. Just over a week later, Boulogne and Calais had fallen. Churchill knew that the British, Belgian, and French armies were facing imminent disaster.

Premier Reynaud, in a state of alarm, was in London on 26 May 1940 to discuss whether the Allies should now consider negotiating with Hitler as soon as possible. Within a matter of weeks, the Belgian and French armies had collapsed leaving the British Expeditionary Force completely trapped at Dunkirk. Attlee and Greenwood supported Churchill's desire to fight on in the face of Halifax's calls for a settlement with Hitler. That day, Churchill authorised Operation Dynamo, the evacuation of the BEF, but did not tell Reynaud. Belgium surrendered on 28 May, opening up Dunkirk's eastern flank to German attack.

British troops trudging through the streets of Dunkirk towards salvation as a bemused Frenchman looks on. Once the Germans had broken through the Allied defences in north-eastern France, it became imperative that the BEF be saved from annihilation. 'It was my decision,' said Churchill. 'When I made it I had a feeling I was going to be sick.' Dynamo ensured that over 338,000 troops were rescued by 4 June 1940; of these, 141,800 were Allied troops, most of whom were French. That day, he told the Commons, 'We must be very careful not to assign to this deliverance the attributes of a victory. Wars are not won by evacuations.'

To add to Churchill's difficulties on 10 June 1940, Italian leader, Benito Mussolini, opportunistically sided with Hitler and declared war on Britain and France. Shortly after, Italy invaded southern France and bombed British-controlled Malta. Churchill was given a breathing space in North Africa because Italian forces in Libya did not attack British-controlled Egypt until 13 September 1940. In the meantime, on 18 June 1940, Churchill informed the House of Commons, 'What General Weygand called the Battle of France is over. I expect that the Battle of Britain is about to begin. Upon this battle depends the survival of Christian civilisation.'

Churchill had to deal with a less well-publicised second Dunkirk. British forces embarking at Cherbourg. The British 1st Armoured Division withdrew to the port with the Germans hot on its heels. The evacuations continued until 25 June 1940, by which time another 144,170 troops had been rescued. At that point, France surrendered and was partitioned between the German-occupied north and Vichy-control neutral south. Worryingly, a question mark remained over the fate of France's powerful fleet. With Europe conquered, Hitler's remaining problem was to persuade the recalcitrant Churchill to submit to his domination of the continent. Hitler said of the situation, 'The British have lost the war, but they don't know it; one must give them time, and they will come round.'

Churchill's first line of defence after the Fall of France was the Royal Air Force. Fortunately for him, RAF Fighter Command had been built up by Air Chief Marshal Hugh Dowding during the late 1930s. He had brought into service the Hurricane (seen here) and Spitfire, which were supported by a chain of early warning radars. Hitler knew that as a prerequisite for invading Britain or forcing Churchill to the negotiating table he needed to destroy the RAF in the air and on the ground. Dowding's fighters had suffered a mauling over France and now faced a new onslaught.

Churchill in RAF uniform. He had good relations with the RAF ever since his time as Secretary of State for Air following the First World War. He had ensured that the RAF was not subsumed by the Army and Royal Navy and remained a separate organisation. In 1939, he was made the Honorary Air Commodore of No.615 (County of Surrey) Squadron.

The French destroyer *Mogador* under attack by the Royal Navy. On 4 July 1940, Churchill told the House of Commons, 'It is with sincere sorrow that I must now announce to the House the measures which we have felt bound to take in order to prevent the French Fleet from falling into German hands.' The previous day, the Royal Navy arrived outside the French naval base at Mers-el-Kébir on the Algerian coast with an ultimatum for French warships: join Britain, be interned or scuttled. When the French failed to comply, they were shelled and a battleship sunk, and four other warships damaged, leaving 1,297 French sailors dead. The French were furious and horrified by the actions of their former ally.

At Churchill's insistence on 22 July 1940, the Local Defence Volunteers were renamed the Home Guard. One million LDV arm bands had been produced, and these had to be replaced. Armament shortages would not be solved until 1942, when the Sten gun was mass produced. While the British Army recovered from Dunkirk, the Home Guard was very much on the frontline. One of the biggest concerns was fifth columnists and the fear of airborne attack by German paratroopers.

Churchill relentlessly toured Britain's defences and cities in an effort to boost morale. At the end of July 1940, he inspected the coastal defences at Hartlepool in north-eastern England. During this trip, he was photographed with an American-made Thompson submachine gun, made famous by American gangsters during prohibition. In response, German propaganda was swift to accuse Churchill of being a gangster.

Throughout July and August 1940, the Luftwaffe, operating from Belgium, France, and Norway, tried to defeat the young pilots of RAF Fighter Command. The Luftwaffe's bombers launched their first massed assault, codenamed Eagle Day, against the RAF on 13 August 1940. London was accidentally bombed on 24 August, and the following day, a furious Churchill retaliated against Berlin. Eighty-one British bombers were sent, though only twenty-five reached their target. This act was to have far-reaching consequences as Hitler turned his attentions away from the RAF's airfields to Britain's cities.

A German Heinkel He 111 bomber over the Thames, London's East End and the Docklands on 7 September 1940. Hitler changed tactics that month and began attacking Britain's cities, in what became known as the Blitz, ranging as far as Glasgow in the north and Plymouth in the west. This saved the RAF from complete destruction and gave it a much-needed respite from attack.

Smoke pouring from London's docks. The Luftwaffe's attack on 7 September 1940 was so intense that panic swept the country, and the invasion alert code 'Cromwell' was issued. In the confusion that followed, it took nearly four hours to reach the coastal commands. The central players in this unfolding drama were Churchill, General Alan Brooke, Commander in Chief Home Forces, General Andrew Throne, commander of 12th Corps, where Hitler's main attack was expected to fall, and Air Chief Marshal Dowding, CinC RAF Fighter Command. The following day, Brooke observed 'all reports still point to the probability of an invasion starting between the 8th and 10th of this month. The responsibility ... is a colossal one... There is nothing to be done but to trust God and pray for his help and guidance.' The population held its collective breath waiting for German jackboots to hit British shores.

'No one,' warned Churchill in a solemn broadcast on 11 September 1940, 'should blind himself to the fact that a heavy full-scale invasion of the island is being prepared with all the usual German thoroughness and method, and it may be launched now'. Across the English Channel, Hitler gathered his invasion fleet, much of which was comprised of converted Rhineland coal barges. RAF Bomber Command desperately attempted to sink them. Churchill, Brooke and Thorne waited for the invasion that mercifully did not come.

Churchill on Horse Guards Parade followed his bodyguard, Detective Inspector Walter Thompson from the Metropolitan Police. On 12 September 1940, Thompson voiced his growing concerns about Churchill's insistence on staying in central London despite the Luftwaffe's relentless bombing. 'Thompson, the Prime Minister of the country lives, and works in that house,' said Winston, pointing at 10 Downing Street, 'and until Hitler puts it on the ground, I work there.' Winston remained determined not to be driven from the capital and urged the royal family and the government to stay put as well. There was to be no evacuation to Canada.

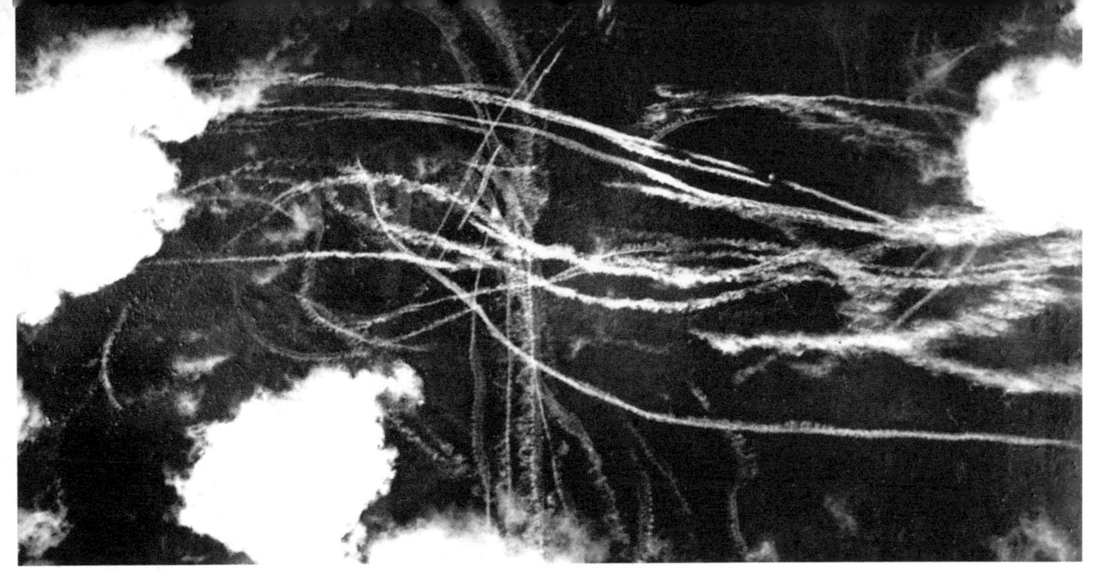

Numerous vapour trails in the summer sky mark out a desperate dogfight. On 15 September 1940, the RAF was almost overwhelmed trying to fend off a massed attack on London. However, the Luftwaffe was beaten off, and this proved a decisive turning point. Two days later, Churchill told the House of Commons, 'The German attacks upon the civil population have been concentrated mainly upon London, in the hopes of terrorising its citizens into submission or to throw them into confusion, and, of course, in the silly idea that they will put pressure upon the Government to make peace. ...

They have, of course, the opposite effect.' The raids, though, continued unabated for the rest of the month.

Churchill and Clementine travelled up the Thames on 25 September 1940 to view the extent of the damage wrought on London's docklands. He was almost reduced to tears and had to be comforted by his wife. The burden of leadership clearly shows upon his face. During the first half of the month, about 2,000 civilians had been killed and 8,000 wounded. Despite this, he was more determined than ever not to abandon London. The Air Ministry encouragingly concluded that the results of Hitler's blitz were 'remarkably small in proportion to the considerable effort expended.' This was of little comfort to Londoners and others up and down the country on the receiving end of Hitler's bombs.

A life underground.
Air-Raid Wardens take
shelter in Portsmouth with
some creature comforts
that include a radio and
stove. The naval base there
made it a prime target.
The Blitz became a war of
wills between Churchill
and Hitler. The latter was
determined to break British
morale and disrupt its
economy, but Churchill
worked hard to ensure this
did not happen.

Shot down Heinkel bombers
became a common sight
across southern England. By
October 1940, the Luftwaffe
had failed to break British
resolve or defeat the RAF and Hitler was forced to disperse the bulk of his invasion fleet.
This marked the end of the Battle of Britain, though the Blitz, which now became a
largely night bombing campaign, would continue into the spring of 1941.

Blazing buildings in the St Paul's area of London. A large attack on 29 December 1940 caused a firestorm that became known as the Second Great Fire of London. Miraculously, St Paul's Cathedral survived all the destruction despite the encroaching flames.

Churchill with the Bishop of Coventry and the city's Mayor visiting the ruins of St Michael's Cathedral in September 1941. Between August and October 1940, the city suffered seventeen small air raids. Then, on the evening of 14 November 1940, it was hit by over 400 bombers. At the time, Churchill faced a dilemma. Ultra intelligence derived from German Enigma traffic indicated that a major British city was to be bombed, and Churchill, it was claimed, deliberately sacrificed Coventry rather than reveal that Bletchley Park was decoding Enigma. However, Ultra did not identify which city was to be attacked, and Churchill thought that London was the target. Coventry was actually a victim of poor intelligence co-ordination within Whitehall. A captured Luftwaffe pilot had warned of a full moon raid against Coventry and Birmingham, but the Air Ministry dismissed this and stuck with its own analysis of German messages regarding their 'Moonlight Sonata'. The city endured another major raid on the night of 8/9 April 1941.

Churchill's Cabinet photographed in October 1941. Standing, from left to right, Sir Archibald Sinclair, A V Alexander, Lord Cranborne, Herbert Morrison, Lord Moyne, Viscount Margesson and Brendan Bracken. Seated, from left to right, Ernest Bevin, Lord Beaverbrook, Anthony Eden, Clement Attlee, Winston Churchill, Sir John Anderson, Arthur Greenwood and Sir Kingsley Wood.

CHAPTER SEVEN

The Widening War
1941–1943

Churchill found himself with much-needed allies against Hitler in 1941, firstly in the shape of the Soviet Union and then America. This necessitated much shuttle diplomacy by Churchill, who met with Soviet leader Joseph Stalin and American President Franklin Roosevelt on a regular basis. Churchill would play his part with aplomb on the international stage, attending numerous conferences to plan the progress of the Allied war effort. America's entry into the war was sparked by Japan's attacks on Pearl Harbour, the Philippines, and British colonial interests in the Far East. This resulted in stretching Britain's resources to breaking point and witnessed the humiliating loss of Singapore and Tobruk, both of which Churchill only just survived. Photographs taken of him during this stage of the war show him looking affable and buoyant. It was he who insisted on clearing the Axis from the Mediterranean before opening the Second Front, much to the displeasure of Stalin.

During June 1941, Churchill attempted to warn Joseph Stalin that the Soviet Union was facing invasion by Hitler. Churchill was well informed thanks to the codebreakers of Bletchley Park, but Stalin refused to listen, suspecting that Churchill was trying to draw him into the war against Germany. At the same time, Hitler reassured Stalin that his troop movements eastward were simply designed to lull Churchill into a false sense of security. Stalin believed him and refused to prepare his country's defences adequately.

On 22 June 1941, the German armed forces stormed through Soviet occupied eastern Poland and into Russia. The Red Army, despite its best efforts, swiftly collapsed, and German troops got to the very gates of Moscow. For a while, Stalin locked himself in his office in the Kremlin, fearing there would be a coup. Churchill, though, had acquired a new and much-needed ally in his war against Hitler.

Despite the entry of the Soviet Union into the war, Churchill desperately needed America's help. Amidst great secrecy, he sailed to Placentia Bay, Newfoundland, aboard the brand-new battleship HMS *Prince of Wales* in August 1941 to meet with President Franklin Roosevelt. The latter arrived on the cruiser USS *Augusta*, escorted by another American cruiser and five destroyers. Both made the journey in the face of the ever-present threat from Hitler's U-boats.

The *Prince of Wales* anchored off Newfoundland. Much to the pride of Churchill, although the battleship had only been completed in March 1941, she had already gained fame. While still in dry dock, she survived an attack by the Luftwaffe in August 1940. Then, in May 1941, she had been involved in the Battle of the Denmark Strait, scoring three hits on the German battleship *Bismarck*. The *Prince of Wales* then escorted a Malta convoy and was attacked by the Italian air force. After repairs ready for the trip to Newfoundland the *Prince of Wales* was escorted by three destroyers, two of which were Canadian.

Amongst Churchill's delegation on the *Prince of Wales* was Canadian Max Aitken, better known as Lord Beaverbrook, on the left. He had moved to Britain in 1910 and gained his peerage seven years later. Beaverbrook initially served as Minister of Aircraft Production during the Battle of Britain, but by this stage was serving as Minister of Supply. His department was responsible for coordinating the equipping of the British armed forces, which were desperately short of everything. Churchill observed, 'Beaverbrook was the only colleague I had who had lived through the shocks and strains of the previous struggle with me. We belonged to an older political generation.'

Churchill and Roosevelt on the *Prince of Wales* on 10 August 1941. Winston later wrote, 'He was the greatest American friend that Britain ever found'. Churchill hoped that Roosevelt would now declare war on Germany and Italy. Instead, he pledged military aid to Russia under Lend-Lease and promised to provide escorts for the British convoys as far as the mid-Atlantic. The pair also issued the Atlantic Charter. Behind them are American admirals Ernest J. King and Harold R. Stark. To the right is William Averell Harriman, Roosevelt's special envoy to Europe. He caused a stir by having an affair with Pamela Churchill, the wife of Churchill's son Randolph.

THE Atlantic Charter

THE President of THE UNITED STATES OF AMERICA and the Prime Minister, Mr. *Churchill*, representing HIS MAJESTY'S GOVERNMENT IN THE UNITED KINGDOM, being met together, deem it right to make known certain common principles in the national policies of their respective countries on which they base their hopes for a better future for the world.

1. Their countries seek no aggrandizement, territorial or other.

2. They desire to see no territorial changes that do not accord with the freely expressed wishes of the peoples concerned.

3. They respect the right of all peoples to choose the form of government under which they will live; and they wish to see sovereign rights and self-government restored to those who have been forcibly deprived of them.

4. They will endeavor, with due respect for their existing obligations, to further the enjoyment by all States, great or small, victor or vanquished, of access, on equal terms, to the trade and to the raw materials of the world which are needed for their economic prosperity.

5. They desire to bring about the fullest collaboration between all nations in the economic field with the object of securing, for all, improved labor standards, economic advancement and social security.

6. After the final destruction of the Nazi tyranny, they hope to see established a peace which will afford to all nations the means of dwelling in safety within their own boundaries, and which will afford assurance that all the men in all the lands may live out their lives in freedom from fear and want.

7. Such a peace should enable all men to traverse the high seas and oceans without hindrance.

8. They believe that all of the nations of the world, for realistic as well as spiritual reasons, must come to the abandonment of the use of force. Since no future peace can be maintained if land, sea or air armaments continue to be employed by nations which threaten, or may threaten, aggression outside of their frontiers, they believe, pending the establishment of a wider and permanent system of general security, that the disarmament of such nations is essential. They will likewise aid and encourage all other practicable measures which will lighten for peace-loving peoples the crushing burden of armaments.

FRANKLIN D. ROOSEVELT

WINSTON S. CHURCHILL

August 14, 1941

The Atlantic Charter set out Britain and America's goals after the war ended. This sowed the seeds for the establishment of the United Nations the following year. Notably Article 6 spoke of the destruction of Nazi Germany but made no mention of Italy. Churchill's concern was that America would seek to apply Article 3 to the British and French empires. However, his main priority at this stage was defeating Nazism and Fascism.

Churchill and Roosevelt again on the *Prince of Wales*, this time with General George C. Marshall, Chief of Staff of the US Army, stood to the right of Churchill. It fell to Marshall to oversee the rapid and considerable expansion of America's military. He was greatly assisted in this by newly appointed US Secretary of War Henry Stimson. Churchill would dub Marshall the 'organiser of victory'.

Surprise attack. After Japan moved into French Indochina in mid-1941, Roosevelt called on it to withdraw and froze all Japanese assets. The British and the Dutch followed suit, and the Japanese lost access to vital oil from the Dutch East Indies. Japanese carrier aircraft launched a surprise pre-emptive strike on the US fleet at Pearl Harbor on 7 December 1941, inflicting 3,435 casualties and plunged America headlong into the Second World War. Of the eight American battleships caught by the Japanese, half were sunk and the others severely damaged. The Japanese also sank three destroyers and damaged three light cruisers. Fortunately for America, its aircraft carriers were elsewhere at the time.

President Roosevelt signing the declaration of war against Japan on 8 December 1941.
He is wearing a black mourning band on his left arm as a mark of respect for those
killed at Pearl Harbor. That day, the Japanese launched a seaborne assault on British-
controlled Malaya and began to push south towards the British naval base in Singapore.
Three days later, Roosevelt signed the declaration of war against Germany and Italy after
Hitler and Mussolini declared war on America.

Churchill's attempts to deter the Japanese from attacking Singapore came unstuck when Japanese torpedo bombers sank HMS *Prince of Wales* and HMS *Repulse* on 10 December 1941 in the South China Sea. Lacking air cover, both warships proved easy prey and 840 crew were killed. This caused an outcry in the House of Commons when Churchill broke the news the following day. It was also a damaging blow to the morale of the British garrison defending Malaya and Singapore.

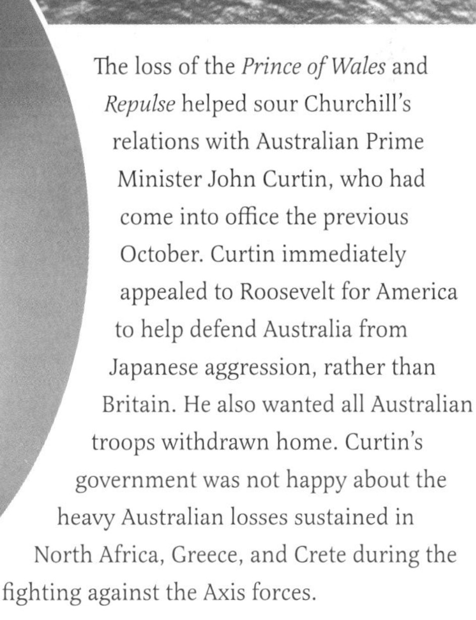

The loss of the *Prince of Wales* and *Repulse* helped sour Churchill's relations with Australian Prime Minister John Curtin, who had come into office the previous October. Curtin immediately appealed to Roosevelt for America to help defend Australia from Japanese aggression, rather than Britain. He also wanted all Australian troops withdrawn home. Curtin's government was not happy about the heavy Australian losses sustained in North Africa, Greece, and Crete during the fighting against the Axis forces.

On 22 December 1941, Churchill and the British Chiefs of Staff arrived in Washington, DC, for a three-week conference with their American counterparts, which was codenamed Arcadia. The following day, a sombre-looking Churchill and Roosevelt faced the press together in the White House.

Churchill addressed a joint session of Congress on 26 December 1941. Behind him are Representative William P. Cole, Jr., (Democrat, Maryland), House speaker pro tem (left), and Vice President Henry A. Wallace (right). Below sits Senate Majority Leader Alben W. Barkley (Democrat, Kentucky). Churchill's speech was well received, but afterwards, he suffered a mild heart attack; Lord Moran, his doctor, told him he was simply overdoing it, fearing the prime minister would be laid up at such a critical time.

Churchill then visited Prime Minister Mackenzie King in Ottawa and addressed the Canadian Parliament before taking a brief holiday in Florida. While in Ottawa, he was photographed by Yousuf Karsh on 30 December 1941 in the Canadian Speaker's chamber of the Speaker of the House of Commons. Known as *The Roaring Lion*, this iconic image came to define Churchill's wartime defiance. In reality, Churchill's scowling expression was sparked by Karsh snatching his cigar from his mouth just before he took the picture. It has since become one of the most reproduced portraits in the history of photography.

Churchill's leadership took another battering when the Japanese rolled into British-controlled Burma and Malaya. Singapore surrendered on 15 February 1942 with the loss of 80,000 Australian, British and Indian troops. Churchill announced on the radio, 'Singapore has fallen ... This, therefore, is one of those moments when the British race and nation can show the sheer quality of their genius. This is one of those moments when they can draw from the heart of misfortunes the vital impulses of victory.' Few listening can have been heartened by such sentiments. Rangoon, the Burmese capital, was lost to the Japanese on 8 March 1942 after British forces abandoned it. India was left exposed and under threat. Indian nationalists hoped the Raj would fall.

British fortunes in North Africa also suffered a major setback. General Erwin Rommel captured the vital Libyan port of Tobruk in June 1942. Churchill was in Washington at the time and was informed that the 30,000-strong garrison had surrendered. The British were driven back to Gazala, just sixty miles from Alexandria. It looked as if Rommel might take Cairo, and a sense of panic swept through the British administration in Egypt and Palestine. Churchill weathered a vote of no confidence in the House of Commons on 2 July 1942. He wrote gloomily, 'Defeat is one thing: disgrace is another.'

Churchill arrived in Moscow on 12 August 1942 for talks with Stalin. He is seen here at Moscow airport, with left to right, Vyacheslav Molotov, the Soviet Foreign Minister, and W. Averell Harriman, the American representative, standing for the national anthems. 'Molotov was a man of outstanding ability and cold-blooded ruthlessness,' observed Winston. 'He had survived the fearful hazards and ordeals to which all the Bolshevik leaders had been subjected in the years of triumphant revolution.' Molotov had been careful never to cross Stalin or covet the top job.

Moscow's military commandant being introduced to Churchill. In the centre, beside Molotov, is Marshal Boris Shaposhnikov, who until recently had been Chief of General Staff of the Red Army. By April 1942, the city was secure from the Nazi threat, having been saved from Hitler by a series of Red Army counteroffensives led by General Georgy Zhukov. This victory not only saved Stalin's regime but also forced Hitler to concentrate his efforts against Leningrad and Stalingrad.

Churchill and Harriman held their first meeting with Stalin in the Kremlin at 7pm on 12 August 1942. Stalin warned them about the German push on both Baku and Stalingrad, and wanted the opening of a Second Front in France as soon as possible in order to divert attention from the Red Army. He was angry when Churchill explained that this could not be done in 1942. Instead, Britain and America intended to clear the Axis forces from North Africa first.

In late March 1942, under pressure from members of his own government, including Deputy Prime Minister Clement Attlee, plus President Roosevelt and Chinese Nationalist leader Chiang Kai-shek, Churchill sent a special mission to India, headed by Labour politician Sir Stafford Cripps, the leader of the House of Commons. 'He carries with him the full confidence of the Government,' said Churchill, 'and he has in their name to procure the necessary measure of ascent, not only from the Hindu majority but also from those great minorities'. This proved an impossible task. In the face of the Indian National Congress and Muslim League's intransigence towards each other, Cripps' mission was doomed to failure from the start. It simply frustrated India's nationalists even further, who took to the streets in widespread protest.

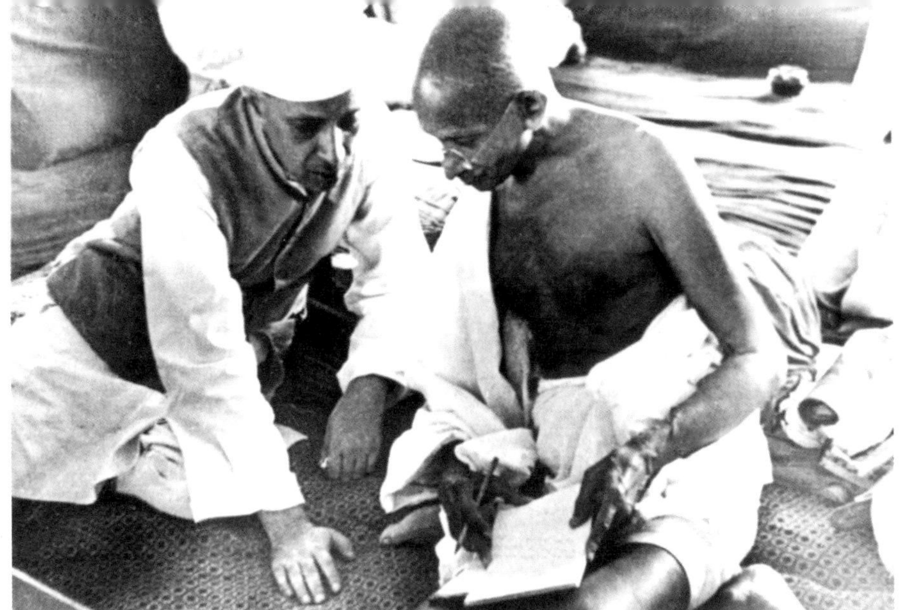

In the summer of 1942, Churchill had to confront Indian Nationalist leaders Jawaharlal Nehru and Mahatma Gandhi when they issued the Quit India resolution. This called for an immediate end to British rule in India and sparked a revolt across the subcontinent at a crucial moment in the war. The Raj authorities conducted mass arrests, and troops were deployed to support the police. For a brief moment, it looked as if Britain's grasp on India might slip.

Fortunately for Churchill in North Africa, the tide began to turn. General Bernard Montgomery, commanding the British 8th Army, after a series of battles by early November 1942, scored a much-needed victory over Rommel at El Alamein. Rommel's exhausted Axis forces had no option but to withdraw in haste toward Tripoli with Montgomery on their heels. Unfortunately, Montgomery did not catch him, and he escaped to fight another day.

Just four days after Montgomery's breakthrough, the US Army, with British support, conducted Operation Torch, landing in Vichy-controlled French Algeria and Morocco. Vichy resistance was short lived and the region was secured for the Allies. Hitler immediately responded by occupying Vichy France. The landings trapped Rommel and the Axis forces, who were squeezed westward into Tunisia, which Hitler moved to secure using a massive airlift of troops and equipment before the Allies could react.

Following Operation Torch, the Allies held the Casablanca Conference in Morocco during the second half of January 1943. As well as Churchill and Roosevelt, the delegates included the Combined Chiefs of Staff (left to right): General Brehon B. Somervell; General H.H. Arnold; Admiral Ernest J. King; Major General Sir Hastings Ismay; General George C. Marshall; Admiral Sir Dudley Pound; General Sir Alan Brooke; Sir Charles Portal; and Vice Admiral Louis Mountbatten.

A close-up of Churchill and Roosevelt at the same press conference in Casablanca. Amongst the many problems they had to deal with was the various competing French factions vying for dominance.

Churchill and Roosevelt, with French military leaders, left to right, General Henri Giraud and General Charles de Gaulle, in Casablanca on 24 January 1943. Roosevelt did not want de Gaulle, leader of the Free French, taking charge, as he viewed him as a potential dictator in the making. De Gaulle, who had enjoyed Churchill's support since 1940, was determined to manoeuvre himself into a senior position within the French leadership.

Roosevelt wanted General Giraud to speak for the French. Churchill, tired of de Gaulle's antics, agreed, 'We all thought General Giraud was the man for the job'. Giraud had escaped German captivity in 1942 and taken sanctuary in Vichy. He had consented to support the Allied landings in French North Africa only if they were conducted by American troops, as he, like many French officers, were resentful towards Britain after Mers-el-Kébir. However, in an uneasy compromise, de Gaulle and Giraud became co-presidents of the French Committee of National Liberation after the Casablanca Conference. Roosevelt dubbed them the 'Bride and Groom'. Giraud, though, soon became disillusioned with all the politicking and stepped down, leaving de Gaulle in charge, much to Roosevelt's annoyance.

British troops in Tunis being mobbed by joyful civilians. About 125,000 German and 115,000 Italian troops surrendered in Tunisia on 12 May 1943. Hitler had steadfastly refused to evacuate them before they were encircled. The following day, General Harold Alexander signalled Churchill to inform him, 'Sir, it is my duty to report that the campaign in Tunisia is over. All enemy resistance has ceased. We are masters of the North African shores.' Churchill later declared, 'No one could doubt the magnitude of the victory of Tunis. It held its own with Stalingrad.'

Churchill with his chiefs of staff aboard the SS *Queen Mary* on their way to America in May 1943 for the Trident Conference in Washington. Left to right are Air Chief Marshal Sir Charles Portal, Admiral of the Fleet Sir Dudley Pound and General Sir Alan Brooke. On the agenda was the Allied invasion of Sicily, the date for opening the Second Front in France and the fighting against the Japanese in the Pacific.

A moment of leisure. Two leaders taking much-needed time out during Trident. Churchill fishing with Roosevelt at the president's Shangri-La (Camp David) retreat in Catoctin Mountain Park in Maryland. 'No fish were caught,' noted Churchill, 'but he seemed to enjoy it very much, and was in great spirits for the rest of the day.' They spent a long weekend in what Churchill described as 'a log cabin, with all modern improvements.' Their conversation included Madame Chiang Kai-shek, who was touring the United States.

Churchill being greeted by smart officers of the Royal Canadian Mounted Police at Quebec railway station. Behind him are Clementine and Canadian Prime Minister Mackenzie King. During 17-24 August 1943, he was in Canada for the First Quebec Conference, codenamed Quadrant, with Roosevelt. Stalin was invited, but he did not attend as he refused to leave the Soviet Union for security reasons.

Left to right are Mackenzie King, Roosevelt, Churchill and the Governor General of Canada, Alexander Cambridge, the Earl of Athlone. Although Mackenzie King hosted, he was not involved in the discussions. Roosevelt rather ungenerously vetoed his presence on the grounds that not all the Allied nations could have representatives at the talks.

Mackenzie King, Roosevelt and Churchill holding a press conference on 18 August 1943 in Quebec. Behind the scenes, Churchill and Roosevelt signed the secret Quebec Agreement in which they undertook to coordinate their efforts to develop the atom bomb.

The three leaders with the Combined Chiefs of Staff. Standing left to right: General H.H. Arnold, Chief of US Air Forces; Air Chief Marshal, Sir Charles Portal; General Sir Alan Brooke, Chief of the Imperial General Staff; Admiral Ernest J. King, Chief of US Naval Forces, Field Marshal Sir John Dill, Chief of Joint Staff Mission, Washington, DC; General George C. Marshall, Chief of Staff, US Army; Sir Dudley Pound, Admiral of the Fleet and First Sea Lord; Admiral W.D. Leahy, Chief of Staff to the US Commander in Chief of the Navy. They agreed that the invasion of France with Operation Overlord would be scheduled for 1 May 1944. Before that, it was agreed to invade mainland Italy in September 1943. This decision did not please Stalin.

Churchill wowing the crowds and the press outside City Hall in Quebec. Mackenzie King is just behind him. Like the Americans, the Canadians generously took him to their hearts.

Another press conference held in Quebec on 23 August 1943. Behind Roosevelt, Mackenzie King and Churchill; seated on the wall are, left to right, Foreign Secretary Anthony Eden, Minister of Information Brendan Bracken, and Presidential adviser Harry Hopkins. While Roosevelt and Mackenzie King appear in a jovial mood, Churchill looks visibly tired.

Chinese Nationalist leader Chiang Kai-shek, Roosevelt and Churchill at the Cairo
Conference in late November 1943. Their discussions centred around the fate of the
Japanese Empire at the end of the war. They issued the Cairo declaration calling for the
restoration of Japanese-occupied Formosa (Taiwan), Manchuria and the Pescadores (Penghu)
islands to China. Japanese-occupied Korea was to become independent in due course.

Churchill was captivated by Chiang's wife, seated on the right. On 26 November
1943, he wrote to Clementine, 'I got on excellently with Madame Chiang Kai-shek
and I withdraw all unfavourable remarks which I may have made about her.'
Roosevelt had invited her to meet him and Churchill in May for lunch at the
White House, but she had snubbed them, refusing to leave New York.

Madame Chiang also captivated Winston's daughter, Sarah, who was accompanying him. She wrote to her mother, 'Papa was impressed by her — and there is no doubt that she is far and away the best interpreter!' Lord Moran, Churchill's doctor, recalled, 'Madame brought Chiang Kai-shek to dine with the P.M. She acted as interpreter; without her, things would have dragged.'

Although wartime propaganda claimed, 'One for all and all for one' with Chiang Kai-shek and Churchill standing shoulder to shoulder, Britain and China had very different agendas in the war against Japan. Churchill remained unimpressed by Chiang, who he did not view as an equal. Nor did he share Roosevelt's faith in Chiang as the man to unite China in the face of Mao Zedong's Communists. Churchill did not view China as a great power and felt it could cause trouble for the British Empire.

Churchill's next conference was in Tehran from 28 November to 1 December 1943. This was the first meeting of the 'Big Three' — Churchill, Roosevelt, and Stalin. The latter's goal was to finally get a firm commitment from America and Britain for the opening of the Second Front. They also discussed Iran, which had been occupied by the Allies to open up a supply route to the Soviet Union, and Turkey, which they wanted to join the Allied cause. Back row: General H.H. Arnold, Chief of the US Army Air Force; General Alan Brooke, Chief of the Imperial General Staff; Admiral Cunningham, First Sea Lord; Admiral William Leahy, Chief of Staff to President Roosevelt.

'This was a memorable occasion in my life,' Churchill remarked of the Tehran conference. 'On my right sat the President of the United States, on my left the master of Russia. Together we controlled a large preponderance of the naval and three-quarters of all air forces in the world, and could direct armies of nearly twenty millions of men.' The problem he faced was that they all had competing goals that were ultimately all about national self-interest.

CHAPTER EIGHT

D-Day and Beyond

1944

The opening of the Second Front in France in June 1944 would see Churchill increasingly sidelined in terms of being the driving force behind Allied strategy. The rapid and remarkable American buildup ensured that they inevitably became the senior partners. His efforts to influence Operations Overlord and Dragoon proved nugatory. This, in many ways, meant that Churchill was relegated to the role of being a war tourist — photographs show that this was something he thoroughly enjoyed. Rather than staying in London, the urge to be involved in the action ensured that he was constantly visiting Allied commanders in France and Italy.

Smiling for the cameras. Churchill with the Allied Supreme Commander General Dwight Eisenhower during a tour of the D-Day preparations in Britain in May 1944. 'Let me tell you what General Eisenhower has meant to us,' wrote Churchill. 'In him we have had a man who set the unity of the Allied Armies above all nationalistic thoughts. In his headquarters, unity and strategy were the only reigning spirits.' Fortunately, Eisenhower was a good diplomat, as he did not always find Churchill easy to work with. Winston's habit of meddling was not appreciated by Eisenhower or indeed, General Montgomery, who was appointed to command the assault force designated the 21st Army Group.

Much to the alarm of Churchill, Eisenhower and Montgomery, Hitler sent Field Marshal Erwin Rommel to shake up the defences of the so-called Atlantic Wall in anticipation of the opening of the Second Front in 1944. Rommel, after his exploits in France and North Africa, was a battle-hardened commander who could bring a lot of experience to bear. He soon embarked on a whirlwind of activity to the extent that one of his commanders grumbled, 'Rommel is a fanatic'. He set about strengthening coastal defences while flooding and mining great swathes of the Normandy countryside, little realising this was where the Allies had chosen to land.

Although Churchill supported Operation Overlord, he increasingly began to worry that it would be a blood bath and sought alternative locations to Normandy. No doubt his concerns were fuelled by the disaster at Gallipoli. Nonetheless, D-Day finally took place despite the weather on 6 June 1944 and proved a remarkable success with Allies swiftly developing a bridgehead despite Rommel's best efforts.

Montgomery and Eisenhower, the architects of Operation Overlord, pose for the cameras. For seven months in 1944, Eisenhower had to endure unrelenting pressure from Churchill and Monty as they sought to strip away resources from Operation Dragoon, to divert it or cancel it altogether. This was to take place in the south of France and coincide with D-Day. Due to a lack of resources, Dragoon was delayed until mid-August 1944. Churchill did not support Dragoon because it weakened the Allied effort in Italy, and Montgomery felt more resources should be allocated to Normandy.

Off to war. Just six days after D-Day, Churchill sailed from Portsmouth on the destroyer HMS *Kelvin* to visit General Montgomery's headquarters. He was accompanied by Field Marshal Alan Brooke, who had been promoted in January 1944, Field Marshal Jan Smuts, the African prime minister and Rear Admiral W.E. Parry.

Once at Montgomery's headquarters, there was the obligatory photo opportunity. Left to right: Lieutenant General Miles Dempsey, commander of the British 2nd Army, Brooke, Churchill, Montgomery and Smuts. Monty had warned Churchill that it was not a hundred per cent safe to visit the bridgehead due to German bombing and snipers. When they arrived, Smuts declared, 'I smell boche' and a terrified teenage German soldier was dragged from some nearby bushes not 50 yards from Churchill and Smuts.

On the first attempt at this photo shoot, both Brooke and Churchill were distracted by something and ended up looking the wrong way at the crucial moment.

Montgomery and his VIPs were then completely distracted by Allied fighters chasing off the Luftwaffe. Although the Allies had overwhelming air superiority on 8 June 1944, up to sixty German fighter-bombers had attacked the Allies' bridgehead in four waves. Fortunately for Montgomery, Churchill and his entourage only stayed the day and returned home unscathed. Shortly after, the British suffered a setback west of Caen at Villers-Bocage when the advance of the British 7th Armoured Division was blunted by a handful of powerful German Tiger tanks.

Even before the Dieppe raid in 1942, Churchill had appreciated the need for pre-fabricated harbours to support D-Day. In a memo to Lord Mountbatten, Chief of Combined Operations, he had instructed that they would need piers that 'must float up and down with the tide; the anchoring problem must be mastered.' This idea led to the building of artificial harbours codenamed Mulberry that were towed across the English Channel following the landings. The American Mulberry was to be deployed off Omaha Beach, and the British one off Gold Beach. Just 12 days after D-Day, a terrible storm blew up ravaging the English Channel and smashing the American harbour.

Churchill discussing the plans for Mulberry B with Captain H. Hickling, commander naval forces Arromanches. Winston flew to Cherbourg on 20 July 1944 to see the American bridgehead and then sailed to the British sector. 'I went aboard the cruiser *Enterprise*, where I remained for three days,' he wrote, 'making myself thoroughly acquainted with the whole working of the harbour'. This Mulberry was the responsibility of Captain C.H. Petrie, Royal Navy and Brigadier A.E.M. Walter, Royal Engineers.

Against advice, Churchill insisted on visiting his field commanders on the battlefield. General Montgomery is indicating enemy positions near Caen on a map held by General G. G. Simonds, the commander of the 2nd Canadian Corps, on 22 July 1944. Lieutenant General Dempsey looks on. Montgomery had just conducted an unsuccessful offensive to the east of Caen known as Operation Goodwood in an effort to break through the in-depth German defences. His two armoured divisions thrown against these suffered heavy losses.

'On my last day at Arromanches I visited Montgomery's headquarters, a few miles inland,' recounts Churchill. 'The Commander-in-Chief was in the best of spirits on the eve of his largest operation.' The Canadians were about to capture the contested high ground to the south of Caen with Operation Spring, while the Americans were about to break out of their Normandy bridgehead just west of St Lô with Operation Cobra. The pair visited the ruins of Caen, and then Churchill was flown over British positions. Regarding Montgomery, he observed, 'This vehement and formidable General — a Cromwellian figure — austere, severe, accomplished, tireless — his life given to the study of war, who has attracted to himself in an extraordinary degree the confidence and devotion of the Army.'

Another field trip. On 7 August 1944, Churchill visited the headquarters of Lieutenant General Omar Bradley, commander of the US 12th Army Group in Normandy. He arrived wearing his RAF air commodore uniform. 'The General welcomed me cordially,' noted Churchill, 'but I could feel there was great tension, as the battle was at its height … I therefore cut my visit short.' German panzers had just launched a counterattack at Mortain, which was threatening to cut off the American breakout into Brittany. At the same time, British, Canadian and Polish troops were attacking along the Caen-Falaise road in an effort to capture Falaise.

Brooke, Eisenhower and Churchill. The latter kept lobbying Eisenhower to shift Operation Dragoon from the south of France to Brittany or somewhere along the English Channel. Captain Harry Butcher, Eisenhower's American naval aide, recalled the acrimonious meeting between the two on 7 August 1944: 'Ike said no, continued saying no all afternoon ... Ike argued so long and patiently that he was practically limp when the PM departed'. Eisenhower later recalled, 'As usual, the Prime Minister pursued the argument up to the very moment of execution. As usual, also, the second that he saw he could not gain his own way, he threw everything he had into support of the operation.'

General Mark W. Clark, far right, commander of the US 5th Army in Italy, agreed with Churchill. He saw Dragoon as 'one of the outstanding political mistakes of the war.' However, Clark was mired in controversy after being distracted by the liberation of Rome, which permitted two German armies to escape north and establish a new defensive line.

Despite his opposition to Dragoon, which was conducted on 15 August 1944, Churchill watched the landings from onboard the destroyer HMS *Kimberley*. He grumbled, 'One of my reasons for making public my visit was to associate myself with this well-conducted but irrelevant and unrelated operation.' Churchill was right, as most of the better German divisions in the south of France had already been redeployed north to Normandy.

Following an intense Allied air and naval bombardment, which included the guns of the cruiser USS *Philadelphia*, Churchill noted, 'As far as I could see or hear, not a shot was fired either at the approaching flotillas or on the beaches. The Battleships had now stopped firing, as there seemed to be nobody there.' He branded the landings as 'rather dull.' This actually was a good thing, as casualties were light and American and French divisions were soon pushing inland on the heels of the retreating Germans.

Naples and Rome were Churchill's next ports of call, with visits to Field Marshal Sir Harold Alexander, the Supreme Allied Commander in the Mediterranean and General Clark. He saw Alexander first in Siena on 17 August 1944. Two days later, he travelled to Castiglioncello with Clark to visit the US 34th Infantry Division. There, he was presented with a bouquet by a young Italian girl.

The Americans ensured that Winston had some fun. 'A pair of new 9-inch guns had just been mounted, and I was asked to fire the first shot,' wrote Churchill with schoolboy enthusiasm. 'Everyone stood clear — I tugged a lanyard — there was a loud bang and a great recoil, and the observation post reported that the shell had hit its mark.'

One for the folks back home. Winston and Clark being greeted by US Army nurses from 8th Evacuation Hospital near Cecina. Allied strategy in France continued to be an issue of contention. Clark made it clear he remained unhappy about US 5th Army being stripped to support Operation Dragoon. Churchill wrote, 'The General seemed embittered that his army had been robbed of what he thought — and I could not disagree — was a great opportunity.' Churchill then returned to Siena and flew to Rome for further meetings.

Churchill had the pleasure of inspecting his old regiment, the 4th Queen's Own Hussars, at Loreto airfield in Italy on 25 August 1944. He had been made Honorary Colonel of the Regiment in 1941 and delighted in wearing his regimental uniform when the occasion warranted. The 4th Queen's had seen action in Greece and North Africa, most notably at El Alamein and then took part in the Italian campaign with the British 1st Armoured Division.

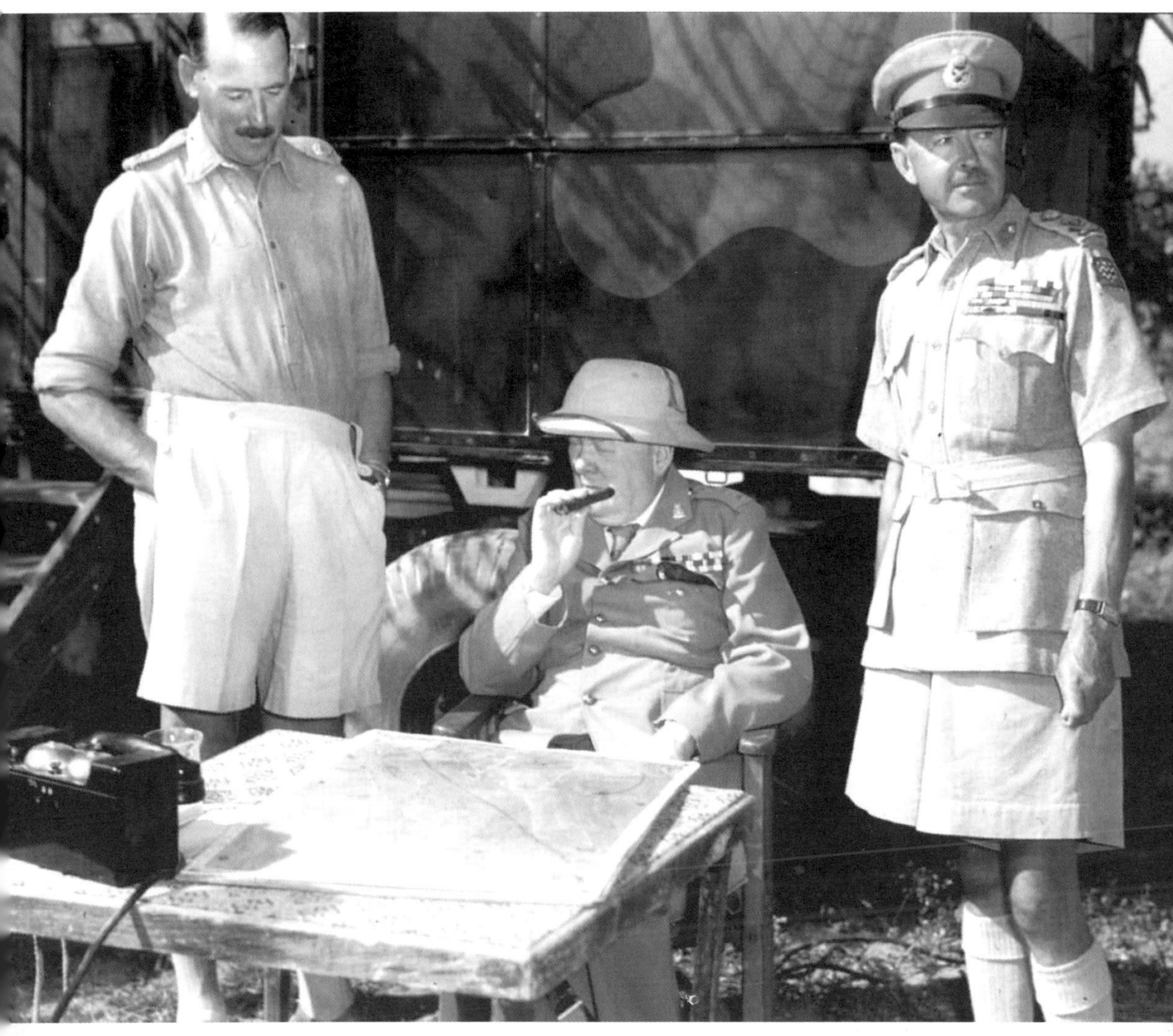

Churchill being briefed at the headquarters of Lieutenant General Sir Oliver Leese, the commander of the British 8th Army in Italy, on 26 August 1944. Alexander is on the right. 'Winston was always bothering me to take him up to the front to see a battle,' recalled Alexander, 'and so far I had dodged his requests because a trip would have been too much of a risk. But now he was more insistent than ever, and I thought, well, after all, we have practically won the war at last.' He took Churchill to a farmhouse overlooking a valley up which British tanks were pushing under German fire. 'Winston saw it all like a demonstration, and was as happy as the proverbial sand-boy,' adds Alexander. The latter was about to launch Operation Olive, designed to cut through the German Gothic Line and capture Rimini.

The Second Quebec Conference was held between 12-16 September 1944. Again, Mackenzie King acted as host but did not attend the discussions between Churchill and Roosevelt. This get-together was dubbed Octagon 2. Left to right: the Governor General of Canada, Alexander Cambridge, the Earl of Athlone, Roosevelt, Churchill, and Mackenzie King. Amongst the topics under consideration were the Allied occupation zones in Germany and plans to drop the atomic bomb on Japan.

CHAPTER NINE

Victory & Rejection

1945

The first half of 1945 proved to be a swan song for Churchill's wartime leadership. The gathering of the Big Three in Yalta in February saw them deciding the fate of Germany and Japan. Churchill was then in Germany in March for the historic Rhine Crossing, which he had to be prevented from taking part in. The death of Roosevelt saw the loss of his key political ally against Stalin. After Germany's surrender, Churchill attended the Potsdam conference only to lose the general election before it finished. Japan's surrender in mid-August finally brought the Second World War to an end. Churchill, though, was out of office.

The Big Three met at Yalta in the Crimea in early February 1945 for their last important conference before the defeat of Nazi Germany. In advance, Roosevelt and Churchill, with their daughters Anna Boettiger and Sarah Churchill, got together aboard the heavy cruiser USS *Quincy* moored in Malta's magnificent Grand Harbour. By that stage, Roosevelt was ailing and looked gaunt and frail. This, though, did not stop him enjoying a cigarette. Sarah reported to her mother, 'It was quite obvious that he was a very sick man. His appearance gravely distressed my father and, indeed everyone.' In contrast, Winston tried to sound positive in a message to Clementine, claiming, 'My friend has arrived in the best of health and spirits.'

Churchill and Roosevelt met twice during their Malta conference and took several took meals together. Winston wanted to agree on a common approach to dealing with Stalin, but much to his frustration, nothing was settled. Roosevelt's health was blamed for this, and it signalled an end to the easy-going relationship the two men had previously enjoyed during the war.

The British and American delegations flew to the Crimea on 3 February 1945. Such was the destruction wrought on the region's cities by Hitler's invasion and occupation that Churchill called it the 'Riviera of Hades'. Neither the British nor the American delegations were happy to be there, especially as they landed so far from the city of Yalta and had to endure a long, tiring drive.

Behind the Big Three stand, from left to right, Field Marshal Sir Alan Brooke, Fleet Admiral Ernest King, USN, Fleet Admiral William D. Leahy, USN, General George C. Marshall, Chief of Staff of the US Army and Major General Laurence S. Kuter. Discussions on the fate of Poland, now with a Soviet installed government, proved wholly unsatisfactory in the face of Stalin's intransigence. Roosevelt, in a secret session with Stalin, agreed that the Soviet Union, in return for attacking Japanese-occupied Manchuria, could have the southern half of Sakhalin Island, the Kuril Islands, the port of Dalian, and Port Arthur.

Visible in this shot in Yalta, left to right are British Foreign Minister Anthony Eden and his Soviet counterpart, Foreign Minister Vyacheslav Molotov, Field Marshal Brooke, Admiral of the Fleet Sir Andrew Cunningham, RN, Marshal of the RAF Sir Charles Portal (standing behind Churchill), General Marshall, and Fleet Admiral Leahy. Roosevelt struggled to concentrate, such was his waning health, but in a letter to his wife Eleanor, he claimed, 'I am a bit exhausted but really all right.' Churchill noted, 'His captivating smile, his gay and charming manner, had not deserted him, but his face had a transparency ... and often there was a faraway look in his eyes.'

Churchill visiting the east bank of the Rhine on 25 March 1945, with behind him,
left to right, General Simpson, commander of the US 9th Army, Field Marshals Booke
and Montgomery. Churchill, always with an eye on historic moments, could not resist
being present for the Allied assault across the river. He flew in secret to Montgomery's
headquarters near Velno to watch the beginning of both Operations Plunder and
Varsity on 24 March. The following day, he and Montgomery arrived at Eisenhower's
headquarters. After lunch they went to a house on the Rhine to look at a quiet German
sector. Once Eisenhower had left to see General Bradley, the pair could not resist
crossing with a group of American officers, remaining in enemy territory for thirty
minutes. 'This is no place for the PM,' grumbled Simpson in alarm to Montgomery.
'I'd hate to have anything happen to him in my area!'

Churchill clambering up onto the wrecked railway bridge at Wesel on the Rhine on 25 March 1945. Once he was up on the bridge, German artillery began dropping shells into the river either side of it. When these began to land on the nearby road, his entourage pleaded with him to come down. General Simpson called for him 'to come away.' Brooke recalled, 'It was a sad wrench for him; he was enjoying himself immensely! However, he came away more obediently than I expected.'

The following day, Churchill was taken for a ride along the Rhine in a Buffalo amphibious assault vehicle. Behind him, left to right, are Field Marshal Brooke and General Dempsey, while Field Marshal Montgomery is seated at the back on the far right.

Churchill's close wartime friend and staunch ally, President Roosevelt, died on 12 April 1945. This image was taken the day before his death. For Winston, it was grievous news, and he was greatly distressed. Five days later, he paid tribute to Roosevelt in the House of Commons, 'I conceived an admiration for him as a statesman, a man of affairs, and a war leader.' His death would have immediate ramifications. 'He was a staunch friend of the country,' wrote King George VI, 'and Winston will feel his loss most of all in his dealings with Stalin.' Churchill later added, 'He was the greatest American friend that Britain ever found.' For Winston, it meant dealing with a new American leader, Harry Truman, who was sworn in as president in the Cabinet Room at the White House a few hours after Roosevelt's death.

Stalin's Red Army commenced its assault on Berlin on 21 April 1945. Hitler took his own life in the Führer bunker nine days later, and the remains of Berlin's garrison laid down their arms on 2 May after the Reichstag was stormed. Churchill recorded, 'The instrument of unconditional surrender was signed by [US] Lieutenant General Bedell Smith and [German] General Jodl, with French and Russian officers as witnesses, at 2.41 a.m. on May 7. Thereby, all hostilities ceased at midnight on May 8.' The signing took place in the French city of Reims, but this was not sufficient for Stalin.

Separately, Field Marshal Wilhelm Keitel, Chief of the German Armed Forces, signed
the unconditional surrender at Marshal Zhukov's Red Army headquarters in Berlin on 8
May 1945. Churchill recorded, 'The formal ratification by the German High Command
took place in Berlin under Russian arrangements ... Air Chief Marshal Tedder signed
on behalf of Eisenhower, Marshal Zhukov for the Russians, and Field Marshal Keitel for
Germany.' This became the official Victory in Europe Day.

Churchill broadcast to the nation on VE Day. He announced, 'The German war is
therefore at an end. ... Our gratitude to our splendid allies goes forth from all our hearts
in this island and throughout the British Empire.' He then read out the same statement
in the House of Commons. Winston concluded by adding, 'I wish to give my hearty
thanks to the men of all parties, to everyone in every part of the House'. The days of
Churchill's coalition government were now numbered.

Churchill greeting masses of cheering Londoners in Whitehall on VE Day with his signature V for victory. He also appeared on the balcony at Buckingham Palace with George VI and the rest of the royal family. Churchill told the throng of people, 'In all our long history, we have never seen a greater day than this'. However, he cautioned, 'Japan, with all her treachery and greed, remains unsubdued.' Both Britain and America would have to fight on in the Far East and Pacific.

President Truman being sworn in. He had been in office exactly a month when Churchill telegrammed him to say, 'I have always worked for friendship with Russia, but like you, I feel deep anxiety because of their misinterpretation of the Yalta decisions, their attitude towards Poland, their overwhelming influence in the Balkans ... and above all their power to maintain very large armies in the field for a long time.' He then chillingly observed, 'An iron curtain is drawn down upon their front. We do not know what is going on behind.'

Churchill, on 5 July 1945, faced a general election that would bring his wartime government to an end. The count took three weeks to get the results, while the ballot papers from the British armed forces overseas were flown back to Britain. 'Many who voted Labour had the impression that they could vote Labour and still have Winston Churchill,' observed his daughter Sarah. 'This they were to learn was not to be so.'

While still awaiting the election results, Churchill, who now headed a Conservative caretaker government, got together with Truman and Stalin to agree on a post-war Europe in Potsdam, southwest of Berlin. Winston met Truman for the first time on 16 July 1945 at the Potsdam conference. 'I called on him the morning after our arrival,' wrote Churchill, 'and was impressed with his gay, precise speaking manner and obvious power of decision.' Behind the scenes, Anthony Eden had been concerned to learn that Truman was not well versed in international affairs. He feared this would weaken the Anglo-American approach to the Soviet Union.

The Big Three during a more informal moment at the Potsdam conference. The key issues were the partition of Germany into Allied-occupied zones and the unconditional surrender of Japan. Churchill demanded free elections in Poland, but Stalin remained unreceptive. Furthermore, at Yalta, Churchill and Roosevelt had agreed that Russia could advance her frontier to the Curzon Line, which left up to four million Poles on the wrong side of the new frontier. Poland was compensated with German territory up to the Oder-Neisse rivers, which meant moving up to eight million Germans. A gigantic refugee crisis loomed in war-torn Europe.

Smiling for the cameras at Potsdam on 25 July 1945. As far as Churchill was concerned, the talks did not go well, principally because Stalin occupied Eastern Europe and had no intention of relinquishing it. When Truman informed Stalin that America had developed an atomic bomb, the Soviet leader showed no surprise whatsoever. It was agreed Japan would be called upon to unconditionally surrender or face the consequences. As far as the Japanese were concerned, this left them no option but to fight on. Stalin agreed to join the war against Japan by driving Japanese forces out of occupied Manchuria.

Back in London on 26 July 1945, Churchill learned that Labour had won a landslide victory. This meant that Clement Attlee, seated on the left, continued the negotiations at Potsdam and not Churchill. That day, Churchill issued a message to the nation. 'The decision of the British people has been recorded in the votes counted to-day,' he said. 'I have therefore laid down the charge which was placed upon me in darker times.' Many were dismayed and surprised that the electorate had shunned Churchill after all he had done. 'For myself personally,' King George VI said to Churchill, 'I regret what has happened more than perhaps anyone else. I shall miss your counsel to me more than I can say.'

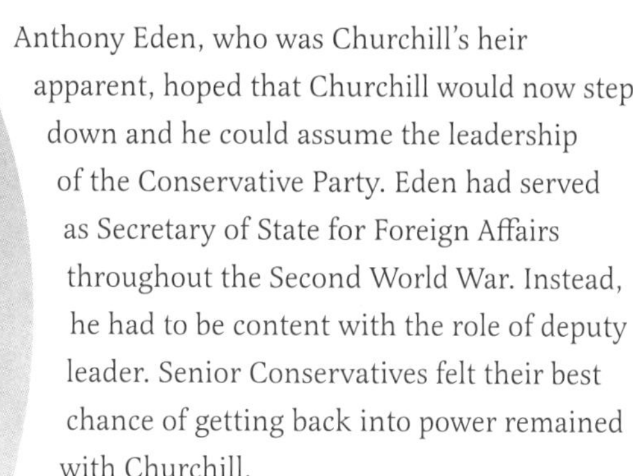

Anthony Eden, who was Churchill's heir apparent, hoped that Churchill would now step down and he could assume the leadership of the Conservative Party. Eden had served as Secretary of State for Foreign Affairs throughout the Second World War. Instead, he had to be content with the role of deputy leader. Senior Conservatives felt their best chance of getting back into power remained with Churchill.

Truman dropped the atomic bomb on the Japanese city of Hiroshima on 6 August 1945. When the Japanese did not immediately surrender, a second bomb, on the right, was dropped three days later on Nagasaki. On 15 August, the Japanese Emperor Hirohito announced that Japan was prepared to observe the demands of Potsdam. That evening, Churchill and some of his colleagues dined in London. 'Dinner was something of an unreality to me,' recalled Anthony Eden, 'because it seemed so strange that Churchill was not at the centre of the national celebration instead of dining apart, in a hotel.' The following day, Churchill addressed the House of Commons, 'Our duty... is to congratulate His Majesty's Government on the great improvement in our prospects at home, which come, from the complete victory gained over Japan and the establishment of peace throughout the world.'

Solemn Japanese representatives aboard the battleship USS *Missouri* in Tokyo Bay prior
to signing of the Instrument of Surrender on 2 September 1945. Churchill warned,
'It would be a mistake to suppose that the fate of Japan was settled by the atomic
bomb. Her defeat was certain before the first bomb fell, and was brought about by
overwhelming maritime power.' In Manchuria, the Japanese Army had swiftly collapsed
when attacked by the Red Army, which then rolled into Korea.

General Douglas MacArthur, Supreme Allied Commander Southwest Pacific, reading his speech to open the surrender ceremony, on the USS *Missouri*. The representatives of the Allied Powers behind him, include left to right: Lieutenant General Kuzma Derevyanko, Soviet Union; General Sir Thomas Blamey, Australia; Colonel Lawrence Moore Cosgrave, Canada; General Philippe Leclerc, France; Admiral Conrad E.L. Helfrich, The Netherlands and Air Vice Marshal Leonard M. Isitt, New Zealand. Lieutenant General Richard K. Sutherland, US Army, is to the right of Air Vice Marshal Isitt. Also present was the Chinese representative, General Hsu Yung-chang, and the US representative, Fleet Admiral Chester W. Nimitz, USN.

The Japanese signing the unconditional surrender. Much to Churchill's alarm, Japan's defeat would facilitate the fall of Chiang Kai-shek's Nationalist China to Mao Zedong's Communists and sow the seeds for the Korean War. This would give rise to the 'Bamboo Curtain'.

Post-war Churchill was far from being a man of leisure. Although he was out of political office, he remained head of the Conservatives and a member of parliament. He was about to embark on writing his six-volume history of the Second World War, which was a highly lucrative project. However, his inability to keep out of the limelight or off the international stage meant that it would take him almost a decade to complete it. The books were actually produced by a team of writers and researchers known as 'The Syndicate' working under Churchill's direction. They were first published in the United States to great acclaim.

CHAPTER TEN

The Post-War Years

1946–1954

Despite being rejected by the nation in the post-war years, Churchill remained very active, leading the Conservative Party in opposition to Clement Attlee's Labour government. This was against the developing backdrop of the Cold War. Concerned about the Soviet threat, he gave his famous 'iron curtain' speech in America just before the East–West stand-off over Berlin. In 1951, he became prime minister for a second time and sought to renew Britain's relationship with America. This generated yet more photo opportunities. For Churchill, though, internationally it was a frustrating time.

In October 1945, Churchill was invited to Westminster College, Fulton, Missouri, to give the Green Lecture. Truman endorsed the invitation and offered to host him. Winston decided to go the following year. His only post-war trip to Latin America was to Cuba in early February 1946. He had last been on the island as a young cavalry officer in 1895 before it gained independence from Spain.

During his second visit, he met with Cuban president Ramón Grau San Martín. Churchill, Clementine and their daughter Sarah spent a week sightseeing and were treated like royalty wherever they went.

The Churchills flew from Cuba to Miami on 10 February 1946 and then on to Washington, DC, where they were joined by their son Randolph to be guests of the White House. While there, Churchill discussed his Fulton speech with Truman before heading back to Florida to receive an honorary degree from the University of Miami.

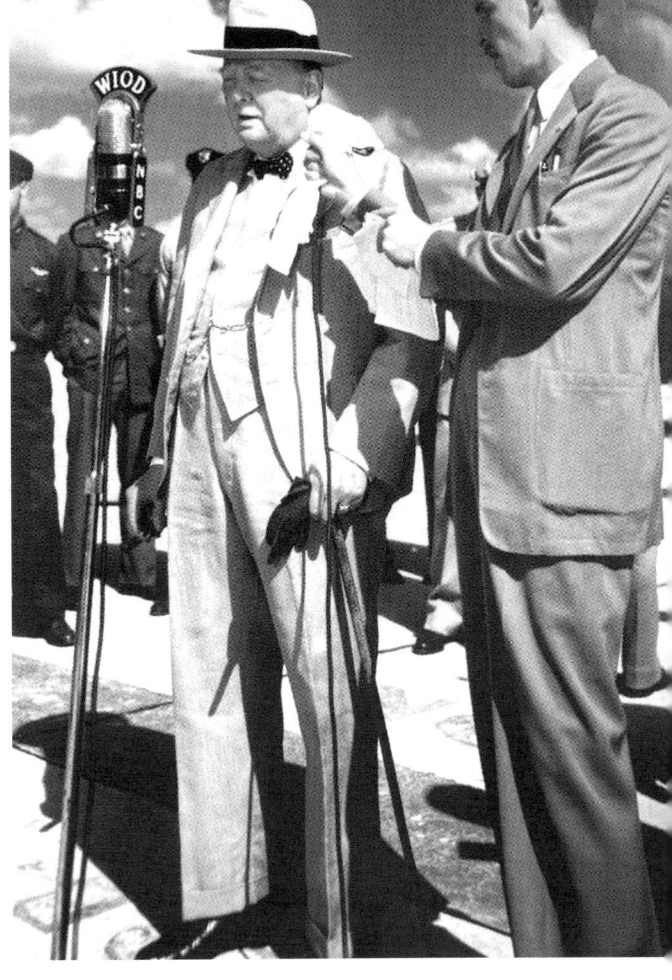

VIP treatment. Churchill met up with Truman in Washington on 3 March 1946, and the pair took the Presidential train to Fulton. Again, Churchill showed Truman his speech called 'The Sinews of War', who told him 'he thought it admirable'.

Churchill, arriving in Fulton, was given the full presidential treatment and was met by a crowd of 30,000 well-wishers. This was much to the irritation of Clement Attlee and his government, as Churchill was no longer prime minister. Churchill gave his speech on 5 March 1946, and warned that thanks to the Soviet Union, an iron curtain had descended across Europe. 'What they desire is …' he said, 'the indefinite expansion of their power and doctrines.'

Churchill inadvertently put Truman in a difficult position, as at the time his 'iron curtain' speech was not well received because no one wanted to hear talk of another world war. Truman even claimed disingenuously that he was not aware of what Churchill planned to say.

Back home, Churchill was exceedingly unhappy at the speed with which Britain withdrew from India and Palestine. As a first step, Jawaharlal Nehru, leader of the Hindu-dominated Indian National Congress, became head of a provisional government on 2 September 1946, but Muhammad Ali Jinnah and his Muslim League refused to cooperate. This consigned India to violent partition.

When it came to Gandhi, Churchill complained bitterly, 'It is alarming and also nauseating to see Mr Gandhi, a seditious Middle Temple lawyer, now posing as a fakir [holy man], striding half naked up the steps of the Viceregal palace to parley on equal terms with the representative of the King-Emperor.' Clearly, Churchill felt that Gandhi was a fraud who should not be given a seat at the negotiating table.

Churchill blamed Lord Mountbatten, who served as the last Viceroy for Britain's rapid scramble from India. Mountbatten, after negotiations with the Indian National Congress and the Muslim League and seeing how British rule was in decay, recommended partition and brought forward the date of independence to 15 August 1947. Churchill never forgave Mountbatten and, for many years. refused to talk to him.

Muhammad Ali Jinnah wanted a separate Muslim homeland in the shape of an independent Pakistan, which was something Churchill supported. He feared that once the British Raj ended, there would be nothing to keep sectarian violence in check.

Churchill held Jawaharlal Nehru responsible for India's bloody partition when the British left. It was divided into three comprising India, West Pakistan (Pakistan) and East Pakistan (Bangladesh). Across the continent, around fifteen million people were displaced, and about 200,000 massacred. Other Indian states, such as Kashmir and Hyderabad, wanted to go it alone, but Jinnah and Nehru ensured that did not happen by sending in the troops. Kashmir was divided between them and Indian forces occupied Hyderabad after brief resistance.

President Truman took heed of Churchill's speech at Fulton. On 21 March 1947, he outlined to Congress what became known as the Truman Doctrine. He announced that America would support global democracy against authoritarian threats, by which he meant the Soviet Union. Historians subsequently saw this as the start of the Cold War.

When Churchill attended the Congress of Europe in the Hague on 7 May 1948, he made it clear that he advocated European unity in the face of the growing Soviet threat. Following his speech, he was given a standing ovation. By unity, he also meant finding a way to bind France and Germany together in order to avoid another major European conflict.

Stalin's blockade of Berlin, which commenced on 24 June 1948 and lasted until 12 May 1949, heralded the opening of the Cold War with a very tense stand-off that threatened to escalate. In response to the Soviets cutting land and water communications into the city, the international community conducted a massive, sustained air lift. Despite the mounting confrontation in the summer of 1948, Churchill, Clementine and other family members still went on holiday in the south of France. The year was notable for another reason: his six-volume history *The Second World War* commenced publication, though it was not completed until 1953.

Chinese Communist leader Mao Zedong with Stalin in Moscow in 1949. That year, Mao's forces prevailed in the Chinese Civil War despite massive American military assistance to Chiang Kai-shek's Nationalist armies. The latter simply collapsed. Churchill was pragmatic about recognising Communist China, remarking, 'If we recognise the bear, why should we not recognise the cub?'

When the Soviet backed Communist North Koreans invaded South Korea in June 1950, it announced that the Cold War was going hot in Asia. Attlee struggled to muster British troops to help the United Nations' forces tasked with driving the North Koreans out. Churchill was very concerned that America would become distracted from its defence of Europe. On 12 February 1951, he wrote to President Truman, 'I have always hoped that the United States, while maintaining her necessary rights in the Far East, would not become too heavily involved there, for it is in Europe that the mortal challenge to world freedom must be confronted.' Truman, though, soon found himself embroiled in a full-scale war in Korea.

WOODFORD PARLIAMENTARY DIVISION

(Comprising Chigwell Urban District and the Borough of Wanstead & Woodford)

PHOTO BY VIVIENNE, LONDON.

The Rt. Hon.
WINSTON S. CHURCHILL, O.M., C.H.

ELECTION ADDRESS

(*Opposite*) Churchill's rather bland leaflet for his re-election as MP for Woodford. In the General Election of 23 February 1950 he hoped that the Conservatives would reverse their defeat of 1945. They lost again but Labour's majority drastically shank from 146 MPs to just 5. Churchill held his seat and Attlee was forced back to the polls the following year.

On 25 October 1951, at the age of 76, Churchill returned to 10 Downing Street as prime minister. This time, the Conservatives managed to win a majority of seventeen seats. Field Marshal Montgomery wrote to congratulate him, saying, 'Thank God. At last we have you back again and in charge of the ship.' Discredited Labour would be stuck in opposition for the next thirteen years.

British troops on patrol in Malaya. Churchill's new government inherited two live wars, one in Korea and one in Malaya. Trouble was also brewing for the British in Cyprus, Egypt, Kenya, and Sudan, all of which would stretch even further the British armed forces. Just as he had done during the Second World War, Churchill appointed himself Defence Minister until Field Marshal Alexander was available the following year to fill the role.

As far as Churchill was concerned the Anglo-American relationship was a priority, so he sailed to the United States to meet with President Truman. Upon arrival in New York on 5 January 1952 he and his entourage flew to Washington, DC, in the presidential plane. Truman was waiting for Churchill as he exited the aircraft. There were smiles all round and a firm handshake.

Churchill and Truman face the press. Truman's preoccupation was Korea, whereas Churchill remained worried as ever about European security.

Truman, with Churchill looking suitably nautical, and British Foreign Secretary
Anthony Eden aboard the presidential yacht, the USS *Williamsburg*, on 5 January 1952,
during Churchill's visit.

Churchill, Eden, US Secretary of State Dean Acheson and President Truman in January
1952. Truman is presenting Churchill with an enlarged photo taken at the Potsdam
conference. Discussions were held on European defence and the global threat posed by
the Soviet Union. Churchill was at pains to highlight that Britain was pressing on with
its costly rearmament programme to help defend against Communism.

Truman hosts Churchill in the Oval Office of
the White House. As always, Churchill had
a cigar in his hand.

During Churchill's second
premiership, he had to contend
with two guerrilla wars fought
against British rule in Malaya
and Kenya. He feared that if the
nationalists triumphed, this
would result in minority rule and
partition for both. Churchill had
Kenyan nationalist leader Jomo
Kenyatta arrested in 1952 on the
spurious grounds that he supported
the Mau Mau rebellion and was a
Communist agitator.

Back in America. Churchill arriving at Washington, DC, airport on 8 January 1953 to say goodbye to Truman, who had lost the US election to Eisenhower at the end of the previous year. He was greeted by a number of American dignitaries, including W. Averell Harriman (second from left), Director of the Mutual Security Agency, and Secretary of State Dean Acheson (third from right).

Acheson shakes hands with Churchill at the airport, appropriately in front of a world map. Averell Harriman and US Secretary of Defence Robert Lovett look on.

Churchill and Truman step outside the White House. They posed together for the news cameras, but no statement was issued. Afterwards, Truman was the guest of honour at a dinner hosted by the British Embassy.

Dwight D. Eisenhower was inaugurated as US President on 20 January 1953. Although Churchill felt that Eisenhower, as a former general would stand up to the Soviet Union in Europe, the Korean War had the potential to escalate because of the involvement of China and the Soviet Union, who both backed North Korea.

Stalin died on 5 March 1953 and was succeeded by Georgy Malenkov. Churchill hoped this change of leadership might ease Cold War tensions. 'When I meet Malenkov,' he said, 'we can build for peace.' However, Nikita Khrushchev was the real power behind the throne and a meeting with Malenkov never took place. The latter was eventually replaced by Nikolai Bulganin and then Khrushchev.

Eisenhower visiting US troops in Korea. Churchill was alarmed when Eisenhower threatened Mao with nuclear weapons if China did not end hostilities in Korea. This, though, had the desired effect, and in June 1953, an armistice was signed.

Winston, in his ceremonial robes of the Order of the Garter, with his son and grandson, for the coronation of Queen Elizabeth II on 2 June 1953 in Westminster Abbey. 'We have had a day which the oldest are proud to have lived to see,' said Churchill with pride in his broadcast to the nation, 'and the younger will remember all their lives.' Her father, George VI, who had been suffering from lung cancer, died the year before from a blood clot in the heart.

Following Queen Elizabeth II's coronation, many in the Conservative Party anticipated Churchill would retire and be replaced by Anthony Eden. However, Eden was unwell, and Churchill remained in post and personally oversaw the Foreign Office in Eden's absence. Unfortunately, on 23 June 1953 Churchill suffered another stroke, which was hushed up while he recuperated at Chartwell.

Fearing Communist subversion in British Guiana in early October 1953, Churchill sent a cruiser and a battalion of troops to install an interim government. He had the colony's left-wing Chief Minister Cheddi Jagan arrested and thrown into prison for six months. MI5 had no evidence that Jagan was under Communist influence and his government's real crime was wanting independence.

Churchill, Eisenhower, and French Prime Minister Joseph Laniel attended the largely unsuccessful three-power summit in Bermuda in December 1953. Churchill hoped that this would result in a big-three meeting involving America, Britain, and the Soviet Union. 'There is a feeling that I am the only person who could do anything with Russia,' he said. 'I believe in Moscow they think that too.' However, Eisenhower made it clear he had no desire for a face-to-face meeting with Soviet Premier Malenkov. 'Russia, according to Ike,' added Churchill, 'was out to destroy the civilised world.' That same month, he was awarded the Nobel Prize in Literature, though he would have preferred the Nobel Peace Prize.

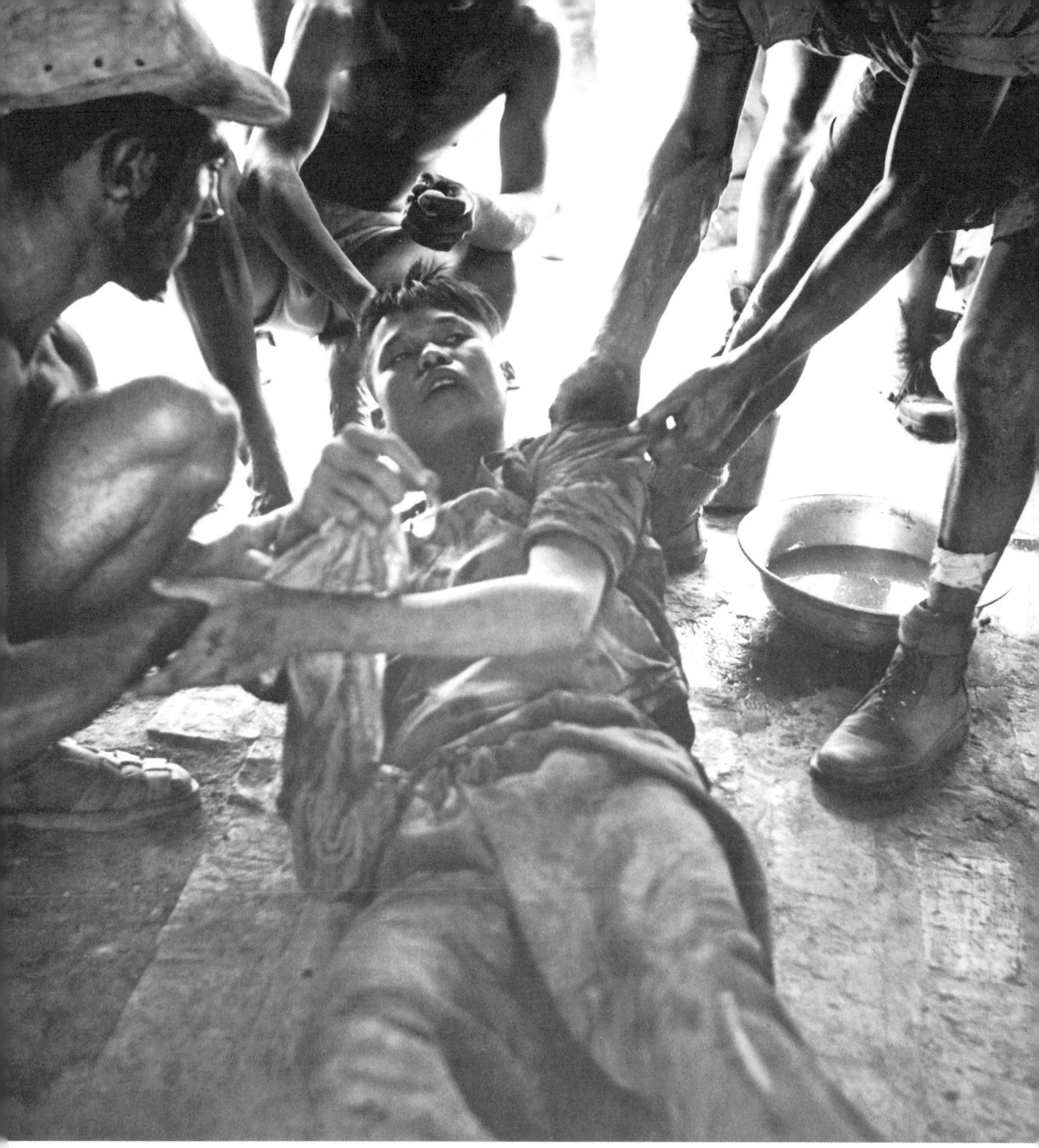

Eisenhower considered using nuclear weapons to save French and colonial troops trapped by Vietnamese Communist forces at Dien Bien Phu in Indochina in 1954. Churchill, however, would not support their deployment, and Eisenhower left the French to their fate. Churchill was annoyed that America was prepared to prop up the French Empire, but did nothing to save Palestine or India. The garrison at Dien Bien Phu surrendered on 7 May 1954, ending French rule in Indochina. This led to partition for Vietnam and independence for Cambodia and Laos.

Anthony Eden at the Geneva conference, which ran from April 1954 to July 1954, trying to defuse the Cold War. Its key tasks were settling outstanding issues from the Korean War and the First Indochina War. Behind the scenes, no one was aware of how close Mao had come to abandoning the Vietnamese if they had lost at Dien Bien Phu.

Churchill arrived in Washington, DC, on 25 June 1954 and was met at the airport by Vice President Richard Nixon. The latter was an ardent anti-Communist. The previous year, Nixon toured the Far East, which included visits to Hanoi and Saigon in French Indochina. He was impressed by Churchill and viewed him as one of a kind.

President Eisenhower greeted Churchill at the White House the same day. Standing behind them in the centre is Secretary of State John Foster Dulles. On Eisenhower's left is a smiling Anthony Eden; Vice President Nixon is to Winston's right. During this visit, they reiterated their commitment to the principles of the Atlantic Charter as the road map for peaceful international relations. It was largely wishful thinking. Four days later, Churchill and Eden headed for Ottawa to meet the Canadian Prime Minister Louis St Laurent and Foreign Minister Lester Pearson.

CHAPTER ELEVEN

A Quiet Retirement

1955–1965

Throughout the Second World War and the immediate post-war year's Churchill's health had not been good. Nonetheless his remarkable fortitude and stamina never let him down. However, in 1955, due to his failing health he was forced to resign as prime minister. Churchill retired, spending time with friends and painting. This, though, did not stop him from fighting a final general election. Images during this period understandably show him increasingly diminished by time, but his zest for life never seemed to wane. When he died in 1965 he was honoured by Queen Elizabeth II with a state funeral.

Winston's Cabinet in 1955. Anthony
Eden, his Foreign Secretary, is seated to
his left. Harold Macmillan serving as his
Defence Minister, is seated on the far left.
Duncan Sandys, Minister of Housing and
Local Government, standing fourth from
the right, married Churchill's daughter
Diana in 1935. Previously, he had served
from October 1951 to October 1954 as
Churchill's Minister of Supply.

Due to his advancing years and ill-health,
Churchill stepped down as prime minister in
April 1955 to be finally replaced by Anthony
Eden. Harold Macmillan became Foreign
Secretary. The Conservatives won the snap
general election the following month with
a sixty-seat majority. Churchill retained his
Woodford seat and remained a member of
parliament. He would spend his retirement
at Chartwell, his London home at 28 Hyde
Park Gate and on the French Riviera, staying
with friends, writing and painting.

When Egyptian leader Gamal Abdel Nasser nationalised the Suez Canal in the summer
of 1956, Churchill supported taking military action with France to regain control.
However, Anthony Eden misjudged the international mood and Britain and France were
castigated and forced to withdraw. Churchill, alarmed by the damage the affair had done
to the special relationship, wrote to Eisenhower saying, 'I do believe, with unfaltering
conviction, that the theme of the Anglo-American alliance is more important today
than at any time since the war.' The Anglo-French attempt to retake Suez was the high
watermark of British military power and imperial ambition.

Churchill and Clementine in London the day before his eighty-second birthday in 1956. This was the only photograph he approved; the rest he instructed be destroyed. Between 1956, and 1958 his much-delayed four-volume *A History of the English-Speaking Peoples* was published. He had started it in the 1930s, but the war got in the way, and he was then sidetracked writing *The Second World War*.

Anthony Eden, humiliated by the scandal caused by the Suez Crisis, resigned as prime minister and as a member of parliament in early January 1957. He was to be replaced by Harold Macmillan. Both men had become prime minister by default just as Churchill had in May 1940.

Churchill was photographed at La Capponcina, Lord Beaverbrook's villa in the south of France, in September 1958, happily painting in the sunshine. This was a lifelong passion and a way of relaxing. 'Just to paint is great fun,' he wrote. 'The colours are lovely to look at and delicious to squeeze out. Matching them, however crudely, with what you see is fascinating and absolutely absorbing.'

These images were taken by Beaverbrook's private secretary and show Churchill working on *Monte Carlo from Cap d'Ail*, which resides in Winston's studio at Chartwell. The following year, he painted two pictures while staying at the Mamounia Hotel in Marrakech. He had last been in the city eight years ago, and the King of Morocco laid on an enormous honour guard for him. He once remarked, 'Trying to paint a picture is like trying to fight a battle. It is, if anything, more exciting than fighting it successfully; but the principle is the same.'

A dinner hosted for Eisenhower on 2 September 1959 in the US Embassy in London.
Winston, who had suffered a stroke that April while at Chartwell, looks half asleep.
Harold Macmillan is second from the right, seated on the arm of the chair.

(*Opposite*) In the General Election held on 8 October 1959, Churchill defended his
Woodford parliamentary constituency and held it once again, keeping his seat in the
House of Commons. Unfortunately, later that month, he had another stroke. Despite
this, in November, he celebrated his eighty-fifth birthday by attending the Commons.

GENERAL ELECTION 1959
WOODFORD PARLIAMENTARY DIVISION
VOTE FOR
ON
THURSDAY,
8TH. OCTOBER 1959

Churchill with his lifelong American friend Bernard
Baruch in New York on 14 April 1961. He was not
up to travelling to Washington, DC, to meet with
President John Kennedy. The following year,
while in Monte Carlo, he broke a hip and had to
be flown home by the RAF. In 1963, President
Kennedy granted Churchill honorary
American citizenship for being 'throughout
his life a firm and steadfast friend of the
American people and the American nation'.

Winston retired from the House of
Commons on 27 July 1964. The following
day, Harold Macmillan told the Commons,
'The life of the man whom we are
honouring is unique. The oldest among us
can recall nothing to compare with him, and
the younger ones among us, however long we
live, will never see the like again.'

Churchill suffered a further stroke on 10 January 1965 and died fourteen days later at the age of 90 at his London home. Bernard Baruch lamented, 'A giant has gone from among us. We are all the poorer for his going. I have lost a cherished friend. Britain has lost her most luminous son, free men everywhere have lost their champion.' In recognition of his achievements he was granted a state funeral by Queen Elizabeth II — who called him 'a many sided genius'. This honour is normally only reserved for monarchs. Notably Churchill's was the last non-royal state funeral, those VIPs since have been accorded ceremonial funerals. Planning for his, dubbed Operation Hope Not, first commenced a dozen years earlier in 1953 after he suffered a stroke. His body lay in state in Westminster Hall for three days, and his funeral was held in St Paul's Cathedral on 30 January 1965. Over 300,000 mourners paid homage to him.

Churchill's coffin was transported from Westminster to St Paul's on a gun carriage draped with the Union flag. With a state funeral, the gun carriage is pulled by members of the Royal Navy, while with ceremonial funerals, traditionally, the carriage is drawn by horses. A state funeral requires an act of parliament and is organised by the Earl Marshal, whereas a ceremonial is organised by the Lord Chamberlain.

The measure of the Queen's respect for Churchill was such that she personally attended, though the monarch does not normally go to the funeral of a commoner. The Queen was supposed to be the last to arrive but came before Churchill's coffin. His funeral was not without incident. President Lyndon Johnson did not go due to ill-health, but it has been alleged he did not go due to Prime Minister Harold Wilson's refusal to support America in Vietnam. The US vice president did not attend either.

Amongst the mourners was Churchill's old wartime deputy and former prime minister Clement Attlee who at 82 was very frail. Attlee said of Winston, 'He was, of course, above all, a supremely fortunate mortal. History set him the job that he was the ideal man to do.'

After the service Churchill's coffin was taken by gun carriage to the Tower of London and then Tower Pier. The dockland cranes along the Thames were dipped in salute. Churchill was carried down the river to Waterloo station and on by train to Hanborough station in Oxfordshire. He was buried at St Martin's Church, Bladon near Blenheim – the traditional seat of the Dukes of Marlborough.

The well-tended graves of Winston and Clementine Churchill at Bladon, the latter died on 12 December 1977. A site of peaceful pilgrimage for many.

CHAPTER TWELVE

Churchill Tributes
1959-2024

Churchill remains one of the most iconic figures of the Twentieth Century. Whether you agree with his politics, you still have to admire his remarkable achievements during a life well lived. Since his death, he has been honoured with numerous statues erected around the world — most appropriately, of course, in London and Woodford. The leading sculptors who rendered his likeness include Ivor Roberts-Jones, David McFall, Vivien Mallock and Oscar Nemon. These tributes serve to honour his long years of public service and his wartime leadership.

Churchill was honoured during his lifetime by his Woodford parliamentary constituency. This nine-foot-high statue was created by Scottish sculptor David McFall and unveiled by Field Marshal Montgomery in the presence of Churchill on 31 October 1959. At the event, Winston lamenting the fate of the British Empire said, 'former systems of government are being thrown aside, and new nations are rising. We wish them well.' Regarding Britain, he added optimistically, 'Let us not lose heart. Our future is one of high hope.' Clementine Churchill had not been happy with the initial design for the statue's head, which was remodelled. She then said, 'It is good', and Winston on seeing it, commented that it was 'very nice'. Woodford was not the first. Four years earlier, a statue of Churchill, sitting by Croatian sculptor Oscar Nemon, was unveiled by the Lord Mayor of London at the city's Guildhall. Churchill, who was the guest of honour, liked it very much. He and Nemon first met in Marrakech in 1951 and became good friends. Nemon's bronzes of Churchill can be found all over the world. Not all tributes were well received. In 1954, the Houses of Lords and Commons presented Churchill with a portrait by English artist Graham Sutherland. It was considered so unflattering that Clementine had it destroyed.

In recognition of the special wartime relationship between Britain and America, a bronze statue of Churchill was unveiled in the American capital, Washington, DC, on 9 April 1966. The plan had been to erect it in time for Winston's eighty-ninth birthday, but it was delayed due to arguments over whether he should be holding a cigar. Standing nine feet tall, it was created by American sculptor William M. McVey. The ceremony was attended by Churchill's son, Randolph. Four years later, a Nemon statue of Winston, hands on hips, was unveiled in the Members' Lobby of the House of Commons.

Although there are many tributes to Winston Churchill located around the world, the most famous by far is the twelve-foot-high bronze statue of him in Parliament Square, London. When Winston was shown the developmental plans for the square by Minister of Works David Eccles in the 1950s, he drew a circle in the northeast corner, saying, 'That is where my statue will go.' Eight sculptors submitted designs and English sculptor Ivor Roberts-Jones was awarded the commission. Roberts-Jones rose to prominence in 1961 when he received an assignment from Lord Beaverbrook to produce a bust of British playwright Somerset Maugham. Three years later, he was commissioned to create a sculpture of British painter Augustus John. Two years after Churchill's death, work commenced on the Parliament Square tribute.

The completed Roberts-Jones statue
was unveiled on 1 November 1973
by Churchill's widow in the presence
of Queen Elizabeth II, The Queen
Mother, the Prime Minister Edward
Heath and four past prime ministers.
Appropriately, the statue faces the Palace
of Westminster, better known as the
Houses of Parliament. The Queen, in
her speech, pointed out that Churchill
had turned down a dukedom because
he wanted to remain in the Commons,
which had been his lifelong second home.

The Parliament Square statue remains hugely popular with tourists, but over the years has been defaced by protestors on a number of occasions and temporarily fenced off or covered up. In 2008, it was protected by a grade II listing, which recognises it as of special historical interest.

Although Churchill had no link to New Orleans, in 1977, a bronze statue by Ivor Roberts-Jones was unveiled in the city. Lady Mary Soames, the youngest of Churchill's five children, who attended the unveiling, said she was very proud that her father 'was chosen to be a symbol of the bond between our two countries and of the mutual passionate love of freedom.' The statue was donated by International Rivercenter, the company that built the Hilton on Poydras Street. International Rivercenter's co-managing partner, James S. Coleman, Jr., served as honorary British Consul for Louisiana. Left to right, Christopher Tidmore of the Churchill Society of New Orleans, the author, and William Allerton, also from the society.

This design by Oscar Nemon was unveiled in Nathan Phillips Square, Toronto, Canada, in 1977. Another Nemon sculpture was unveiled in Halifax, Canada, three years later. Over a fifty-year period, Churchill forged a close relationship with Canada. He first travelled there in 1900, when he was on a lecture tour discussing his adventures during the Boer War.

A replica of the Parliament Square statue was unveiled in 1999 in Winston Churchill Square in Prague, Czech Republic, outside the University of Economics. It was moulded from the original on site, then cast in bronze. A fibreglass replica is also located in the grounds of the Australian National University campus in Canberra.

A small version of the Ivor Roberts-Jones'
statute, cast in bronze, is displayed at
the M.S. Rau Gallery in New Orleans.
It has outstanding exhibits, including a
number of Churchill bronzes. After the
Parliament Square statue was unveiled it
proved so popular that a series of scaled-
down cast versions were produced. This
example is number 132 of 500 created by
the Meridian Bronze Foundry.

This unique bronze maquette,
depicting Churchill in his garter
robes, is Roberts-Jones' original
design for the Parliament
Square statue. It resides in the
M.S. Rau collection. This design
was revised at the request of
Clementine Churchill, who
wanted her husband to have a
more military appearance to
reflect his wartime leadership
— hence the greatcoat.

Six casts of the head and shoulders were taken from the mould used for the monument of Churchill in Parliament Square. This striking artist's proof, at over four feet wide, was displayed by M.S. Rau.

The M.S. Rau Gallery contains another fine, larger-than-life Churchill bronze. This time by English sculptor Vivien Mallock, that was designed as a gift for the US Defense Department from the British Ministry of Defence in 2015. It was dedicated at the Pentagon's Hall of Heroes. This example is seventh in a series of only twelve produced.

M.S. Rau features an example of Oscar Nemon's work called appropriately 'Married Love', depicting a seated Clementine and Winston. This bronze resin sculpture was commissioned by Lady Churchill after her husband's death, and the original stands in the grounds of Chartwell. Another version is located at Blenheim Palace.

A Churchill statue by Oscar Nemon can be found in Churchill Square, Edmonton, Canada, near the city hall, which was unveiled by Lady Soames on 24 May 1989. It was donated to the city by the Sir Winston Churchill Society of Edmonton.

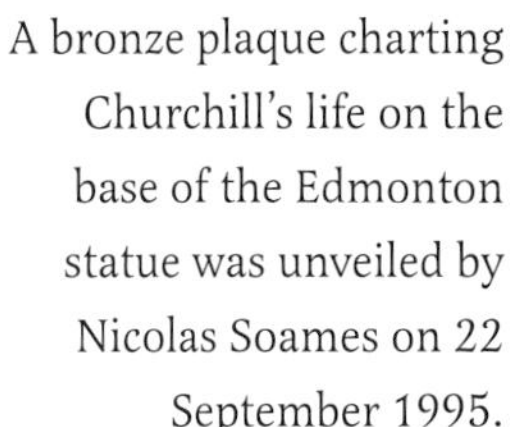

A bronze plaque charting Churchill's life on the base of the Edmonton statue was unveiled by Nicolas Soames on 22 September 1995.

THE LIFE OF

RT. HON. SIR WINSTON SPENCER CHURCHILL
K.G., O.M., C.H., F.R.S.

1874	BORN BLENHEIM PALACE, NOVEMBER 30
1882-92	HARROW SCHOOL
1893-95	ROYAL MILITARY COLLEGE, SANDHURST
1895	CUBA - SPANISH FORCES
1897	INDIA - MALAKAND FIELD FORCE
1898	SUDAN - OMDURMAN, KHARTOUM
1899-1900	SOUTH AFRICA - WAR CORRESPONDENT
1901-06	MP FOR OLDHAM
1906-08	UNDER SECRETARY OF STATE
1908-10	PRESIDENT, BOARD OF TRADE
1910-11	HOME SECRETARY
1911-15	FIRST LORD OF THE ADMIRALTY
1917-19	C.O. 6TH ROYAL SCOTS FUSILIERS
1919-21	MINISTER OF MUNITIONS
1921-22	SECRETARY OF STATE FOR WAR
1922-24	SECRETARY OF STATE FOR THE COLONIES
1929-39	"THE WILDERNESS YEARS"
1939-40	FIRST LORD OF THE ADMIRALTY
1940-45	PRIME MINISTER, FIRST LORD OF THE TREASURY, MINISTER OF DEFENCE
1945-51	LEADER OF THE OPPOSITION
1951-55	PRIME MINISTER
1953	NOBEL PRIZE FOR LITERATURE
1955-64	MP - BACK BENCHER
1965	DIED JANUARY 25TH

IN WAR:	RESOLUTION
IN DEFEAT:	DEFIANCE
IN VICTORY:	MAGNANIMITY
IN PEACE:	GOODWILL

While on holiday on Madeira in 1950 Churchill painted the fishing village of Câmara de Lobos. To honour the occasion, a statue of him sitting at his painting easel was unveiled on 26 June 2019. He had previously visited the island in 1899 when he was on his way to South Africa.

Churchill collectables produced during his lifetime and afterwards, come in all shapes and sizes, including this wartime lighter. It was designed and moulded by Peter Lamda for Tallent and was intended for use in pubs and restaurants. The cigar, which is missing from this example, had a flint which was struck across the metal plate on the base at the front. The lighter was usually produced in plain terracotta colour, though some were painted. This one can be found in the Davidstow Moor RAF Memorial Museum in Cornwall, England.

A small cold cast Nemon-style Churchill bust produced in 1997, nestled amongst his writings.

Churchill busts remain popular, and variations on this particular design are very common and have even been produced as garden ornaments.

One of the most recent tributes to Churchill stands in Calgary, Canada. This was unveiled on 6 June 2024 on the eightieth anniversary of D-Day. He visited Calgary in 1929 as part of a three-month tour of North America that took in most of the principal Canadian cities, including Ottawa, Montreal and Toronto.

The Calgary statue was designed by Canadian sculptor Danek Mozdzenski and was commissioned by the Sir Winston Churchill Society of Calgary. It portrays Churchill purposely striding forward with his signature hat and cane.

Picture Sources

The images in the book have been drawn from a wide variety of public domain sources including the Cape Archive, Dutch National Archives, FDR Presidential Library & Museum, Harry S. Truman Library, Library and Archives of Canada, Library of Congress, National Archives and Records Administration, National Library of Australia, National Library of Ireland, Naval History and Heritage Command, Transvaal Archive, UCLA Library and Wikimedia Commons; plus the author's own picture library. The author is grateful to Brian E. Krapf, Ocean View Group Ltd, the Scott Pick Collection, the M.S. Rau Gallery and Dan Reinbold for their kind assistance with the provision of additional images.

Suggested Further Reading

Arthur, Max
Churchill The Life: An Authorised Pictorial Biography
London: Cassell, 2017

Blundell, Nigel
Winston Churchill: The Pictorial History of a British Legend
Barnsley: Pen & Sword, 2011

Carter, Katherine
Churchill's Citadel: Chartwell and the Gatherings Before the Storm
New Haven & London: Yale University Press, 2024

Catherwood, Christopher
Churchill: The Story of the Greatest Briton in Words, Photographs and Documents
London: Seven Oaks, 2018

Cross, Robin
Man of the World: The Travels of Winston Churchill
Stroud: Amberley, 2024

Delmas, Vincent & Regnault, Christophe
Churchill: A Graphic Biography
Barnsley: Greenhill Books, 2020

Ferrier, Neil, (ed)
Churchill The Man of the Century: A Pictorial Biography
London: Robinson, 1955

Gilbert, Martin
In Search of Churchill: A Historian's Journey
London: Harper Collins, 1994

Gilbert, Martin
Winston Churchill: The Wilderness Years
London: Macmillan, 1981

Krapf, Brian E.
A Churchill Treasury: Sir Winston's Public Service Through Memorabilia
Barnsley: Pen & Sword, 2023

Reed, Phil & Richards, Anthony
Winston Churchill in 100 Objects
Barnsley: Greenhill Books, 2024

Reynolds, David
Mirrors of Greatness: Churchill and the Leaders who Shaped Him
London: William Collins, 2023

Roberts, Andrew
Churchill Walking with Destiny
London: Penguin, 2019

Sandys, Celia
Churchill by his granddaughter, Celia Sandys
London: Imperial War Museum, 2010

Toye, Richard
The Roar of the Lion: The Untold Story of Churchill's World War II Speeches
Oxford: Oxford University Press, 2015

Toye, Richard
Winston Churchill: A Life in the News
Oxford: Oxford University Press, 2021

Tucker-Jones, Anthony
Churchill Master and Commander: Winston Churchill at War 1895-1945
Oxford: Osprey Publishing, 2021

Tucker-Jones, Anthony
Churchill Cold War Warrior: Winston Churchill and the Iron Curtain
Barnsley: Frontline Books, 2024